An Account of Japan, 1609

Roderigo de Vivero

An Account of Japan, 1609

Translated and introduced by
Caroline Stone

Hardinge Simpole

Hardinge Simpole
an imprint of
Zeticula Ltd
Unit 13
196 Rose Street
Edinburgh
EH2 4AT
Scotland.

http://www.hardingesimpole.co.uk
admin@hardingesimpole.co.uk

First published in this edition 2015
Copyright © Caroline Stone 2015

Cover Design Copyright © Zeticula 2015
ISBN 978-1-84382-224-0

To
Paul Lunde
Alexander and James Stone Lunde

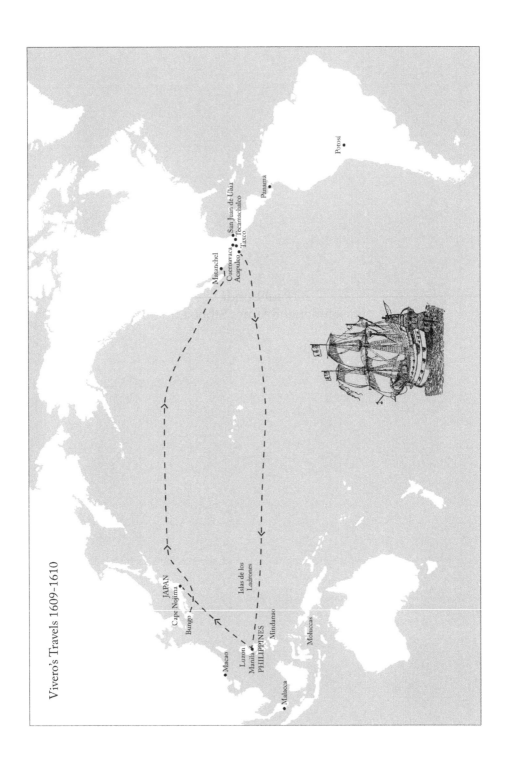

Vivero's Travels 1609-1610

Potosí

Panamá

San Juan de Ulúa
Cuernavaca
Acapulco
Tecamachalco
Taxco

Matanchel

JAPAN
Cape Nojima
Bungo
Macao
Luzon
Manila
PHILIPPINES
Mindanao

Islas de los
Ladrones

Moluccas

Malacca

Contents

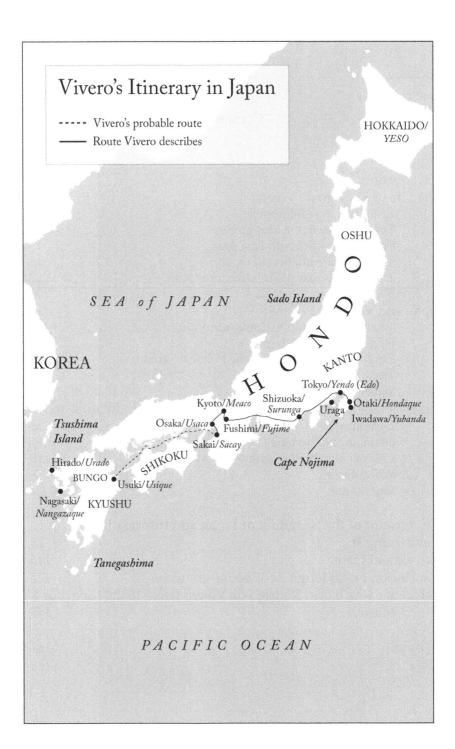

Foreword

This is not intended as an academic translation; it aims to make an interesting text accessible and to provide background information on some of the lesser known aspects of the period. It was chosen in preference to several much more detailed accounts of Japan, particularly by the Jesuit Fathers, for practical reasons, because Vivero, being a military man rather than in Holy Orders, presents a different view of Japan, but also because at the time I was working on the Civilisations in Contact Project associated with the Faculty of Asian and Middle Eastern Studies at Cambridge University and this particular text brings an extraordinary number of different civilizations into contact.

The question of transcription and names is always a thorny one. Where there is a word that is well known in English, such as kimono or samurai, I have used the standard English spelling, reserving the use of long marks over vowels and other signs for words which are unassimilated. Similarly, I have generally used the modern form of place names, giving Vivero's version of them in the footnotes. The exceptions are Edo or Yendo [modern Tokyo] and Miyako [modern Kyoto], which I have left in the original, in part to give flavour, but mostly as a reminder that these cities in the 17th century were completely different from today, not merely in the obvious physical sense, but in terms of their functions and relationship to Japan as a whole. On the maps, Vivero's names are given in italics,

Vivero was neither a scholar nor a great stylist. I have tried to give an impression of his Spanish, which is sometimes confusing in its 17th century formality and the accompanying tendency to interminable sentences, mixed on occasion with very colloquial expressions. Surprisingly little is known about Vivero beyond what appears in his writings and some material in the Archivo General de Indias in Seville. However, his style joins with his opinions to give a clear and memorable impression of his personality – not one that will necessarily appeal to modern readers, but political correctness was not a feature of the early 17th century.

I would like to thank Stanford University Press for courteously allowing me to quote from *Annals of His Time* by Domingo Francisco de San Antón Muñón Chimalpahin Quauhtlehuanitzin, edited and translated by James Lockhart, Susan Schroeder and Doris Namala (2006).

My husband, Paul Lunde, lent, as always, invaluable support, for which I am more than grateful. I would like to thank my sons: Alexander Stone Lunde for his help with the 17th century vocabulary and James Stone Lunde with the Japanese. Let me quickly stress that all errors are my own.

For personal reasons, this book was put together over several years and I would also like to thank the friends in whose houses the work was done – and perhaps even the houses themselves:

It was begun in the home of Ana Maria Pellecer, the Casa de los Cantaros in La Antigua Guatemala.

Continued in the house of Anu Mathew at Philipkutty's Farm, near Kottayam in Kerala.

Revised at the University Library and at various other points in Cambridge.

Completed in the Barrio de Santa Cruz, Seville, October 15th, 2014.

Introduction

The Life of Rodrigo de Vivero [1]

Rodrigo de Vivero y Velasco was born in Mexico c.1564 and died in 1636 on his *encomienda* (estate) at the village of Tecamachalco in the Puebla region. On his father's side he came from a noble Castilian family from Valladolid and his relatives held numerous important positions. His paternal grandfather had married the sister of the future Viceroy of New Spain (1549-1564), Luìs de Velasco, whose son, Luìs de Velasco the younger, Marquis de Salinas, also became Viceroy, twice of New Spain (1590-1595 and 1607-1611) and once of Peru (1596-1604). It was for this reason that Vivero added Velasco to his name, rather than that of his mother, as would have been customary. Unlike his father, who came to Mexico as a child, his mother was born there, from similarly aristocratic stock, and the rich Tecamachalco *encomienda* came into Vivero's family from her.

Vivero was sent as a child to Spain – very much as children were sent home from British India – perhaps about 1577 to escape an epidemic that was raging. He was thus raised at the court of Philip II, probably as a page of Queen Anne. He served on the expedition to Portugal of the great general, Fernando Álvarez de Toledo, Duke of Alba in 1580 and under the Marquis of Santa Cruz, commander of the "Invincible Armada", until his death in 1588, when his place was taken by the Duke of Medina Sidonia, who lacked naval experience.

On Vivero's return to Mexico, he subdued Indian uprisings under his uncle Luìs de Velasco and was called upon to defend the port of Acapulco, under threat from English corsairs. In 1591, he married Leonor de Arellano y Ircio, a descendant of the first Viceroy of New Spain, and in 1592 his son, Luìs, was born.

Vivero filled a number of administrative posts of increasing importance and in 1595 was put in charge of the port of San Juan de Ulúa, which meant that as well as a military background, he also had administrative experience and responsibility for guarding New Spain's ports and trade routes from attack by the predominantly English and Dutch corsairs. In 1597 he requested – perhaps in order to be closer to his family's estates, part of which he had inherited – the charge of the great silver mines at Taxco, and it was granted. This meant that Vivero added a profound working knowledge of the technical and economic aspects of silver production to his other fields of competence and explains both his interest in the question of silver mining in Japan, the other great source of silver in the world at the time, and the chapters dedicated to silver in his *Advice.*

Having given satisfaction in this post, in 1599 he was appointed Governor of Nueva Vizcaya – present day Durango and Chihuahua. This was an important charge, since the area was both rich in silver mines and inhabited by "unpacified" Indian tribes, and Vivero was given a free hand to deal with the situations that arose. It was a six year appointment and for part of this period he was in serious ill-health.

Then, in 1608 he was appointed Interim Governor of the Philippines. The previous Governor had died in 1606, his successor, Juan de Silva, was not ready to leave and another potential Interim Governor had refused the post. Luìs de Velasco then put forward the name of his nephew as a suitable candidate. Vivero accepted at once, apparently not even returning home, and pausing only to make his will at Cuernavaca on February 25th, 1608, before embarking at Acapulco on March 15th and arriving on June 13th. The crossing was fairly standard: a brush with Dutch corsairs and the deaths of 24 men from illness, and on 8th July, he was writing home to the Viceroy.

In Manila, Vivero was both active and effective, especially with regard to the accounts and in driving forward trade negotiations with Japan, which had stagnated under previous Governors (see *The Japanese in the Philippines*), but at Easter 1609, Juan de Silva arrived to take up his appointment, something that Vivero clearly resented, feeling – understandably – that the post should have been given to him. On July 25th, he set out for New Spain and was wrecked on the coast of Japan on September 30th. The texts in this volume relate to his time there.

The years immediately after his return on October 25th, 1610 are shadowy, but his uncle's death in 1614 probably undermined his career prospects – certainly for the post of Viceroy for which he may have hoped, but which never came his way.

In 1620, Vivero seems to have been in Spain putting forward his son, Luìs, as a Knight of Santiago, an honour held by his father and grandfather but, curiously, not by Vivero himself. It was there that he received a new appointment as Capitán General de Tierra Firme[1] and Presidente de la Audiencia de Panamá and swiftly embarked from Cadiz or Sanlúcar de Barrameda. Once again, the post drew on his previous experience, since it was from Panama that the silver from the mines of Potosí was despatched to Seville and consequently defending both port and fleet from pirate attacks was a top priority. The appointment was for eight years – which must have been gruelling ones – and in 1627 Vivero was given the title of Conde de Valle de Orizaba from the area where his estates lay and was allowed to return to his home in Mexico. It seems to have been then that he finally set down his *Relación.*

In 1632, he was summoned from his well-deserved retirement to advise on the defence of San Juan de Ulúa and Veracruz, threatened with attack by Dutch corsairs, and a new appointment reached him shortly before his death at Tecamachalco on December 8th, 1636.

[1] This a very brief outline of Vivero's life. For a more detailed account of his family, appointments, the ms and publishing history of the text, see the excellent Introduction to Juliette Monbeig's edition (see bibliography), henceforth cited as JM.

[2] The Isthmus of Panama and parts of what are now Columbia and Venezuela.

Bibliography

Alvarez, J.L. *"Don Roderigo de Vivero y la destrucción de la Nao Madre de Deos 1609"*, Tokyo: Sophia University, Monumenta Nipponica vol.II, No 2, pp.479-511, 1939

Ariza Torres, Cristóbal, *Datos historicos sobre don Roderigo de Vivero y el general Sebastián Vizcaíno encontrados en el Archivo de Indias*, Madrid: Ministerio de Marina, 1926

Vivero, Roderigo de, *Du Japon et du bon gouvernement de l'Espagne et des Indes*, tr. Juliette Monbeig, Intro. Fernand Braudel, Paris: 1972

Sarabia Viejo, María Justina, *Don Luìs de Velasco, virrey de Nueva España*, Sevilla : Escuela de Estudios Hispano Americanos de Sevilla, 1978

Spain and the Philippines

Although parts of the Philippines were probably known before, the first recorded European contact is usually considered to be March 16th, 1521, by Magellan, who claimed such islands as he saw for Spain. In 1543, Ruy López de Villalobos called the islands of Leyte and Samar "Las Islas Filipinas" in honour of Philip II and the term much later came to be used for the whole region. The archipelago at this date was a patchwork of independent rulers and tribal confederations, as well as the relatively recently arrived Muslim element, which was actively engaged in proselytising and conquering.

On February 13th, 1565, Miguel López de Legaspi reached the Philippines and formally claimed them for the Spanish Crown. He arrived at Manila Bay on the island of Luzon on June 24th, 1571 and chose it as the capital. The unification of the Philippines – apart from the Muslim Sultanates of Mindanao and the highland Ifugao of Northern Luzon, which remained detached and alienated – took place at roughly the same time as the unification of Japan, although clearly under very different circumstances. The fragmented nature of the country made concerted resistance difficult and hence its conquest and conversion was swift and relatively easy.

The Philippines and New Spain were closely associated from the beginning and the appointment of Vivero was only one more link in the chain, the uniting factor being the Manila galleons which transported the valuable and coveted Far Eastern trade goods to Mexico for transshipment to the ports of Spain. The Philippines were governed as a territory of New Spain from 1565-1821, when they were transferred to Spain in the wake of Mexican Independence. It has been postulated that Legaspi, given the shortage of Spanish soldiers, brought with him, among his 500 troops, Central Americans, who settled in the Pampanga region around a native town renamed "Mexico". Large numbers of plants indigenous to Central and South America were introduced into the country at this time and their cultivation remains especially intense in the Mexico region, notably the *chico* or *sapodilla* plantations.

For a variety of reasons, efforts to create local industries were relatively unsuccessful – for example, *piña*, the highly desired textile developed in the Philippines from the American pineapple was never produced in quantities to satisfy demand – except those in Chinese hands. The commercial importance of Manila was, therefore, as an entrepôt, for the Manila galleons, especially in the period 1572-1593, after which pressure from the merchants of Seville and the Council of Portugal severely limited their numbers and capacity. Nevertheless, it was where Japanese and Chinese merchants, who were theoretically forbidden to trade directly (the Japanese being banned from China, including Macao) could exchange Japanese silver and arms for Chinese silks and luxury goods. The Japanese imported vital food-stuffs, horses etc. to the Philippines and were therefore given preferential treatment as regards tax, while their military support of the Spanish on various occasions led to their being treated with favour. Meanwhile, the relative peace imposed by the Tokugawa shogunate led to a considerable increase in prosperity and demand for luxury goods, and the newly discovered silver mines put the Japanese in an excellent position for acquiring them; the problem was access, because of restrictions in all directions by the various governments.

Relations with the Chinese were somewhat different. Contacts were mostly with Fujian, where poor land and population increase had led to a diaspora. The Spanish, concerned at this excessive immigration, theoretically limited the number of Chinese resident in the Parian quarter of Manila allotted to them to 6,000, but this was constantly exceeded, leading to various efforts at expulsion and the massacre of 1603.

The rapid progress made by the colonisers is made very clear in the *Relación de las Encomiendas existentes en Filipinas 1591*, which sets down population statistics for the islands, or at least the main settlements, as well as land holdings and amenities, such as a hospital for the Spanish population and another to serve the needs of the locals. As always, the conversion of the indigenous people was a very high priority for the Spanish conquerors and Franciscans, Dominicans, Augustinians and Jesuits each had their monasteries or houses, as well as churches. The Franciscans attended to the growing Japanese community, while the Dominicans looked after the Chinese, providing schools for the converts' children.

Education – general as well as religious – was a very important part of the colonial programme, especially for the Jesuits, who founded numerous establishments, including the Colegio de Manila in 1590, the Colegio de San Ildefonso 1595, the Colegio de San José in 1601 and the University of Santo Tomás in 1611. As a result of this – and, according to de Morga, an indigenous tradition of literacy – the people of the Philippines has the greatest access to education of any part of Asia. The first officially recognised convent for women in the Far East was the Monastery of Santa Clara in Intramuros, Manila, founded by the formidable Mother Geronima de la Asunción of the Colettine Poor Clares.

Bibliography

Boxer, C.R, *Fidalgos in the Far East, 1550-1770*, The Hague: Martinus Nijhoff, 1948

Gil, Juan, *Los Chinos en Manila*, Lisboa: Centro Cientifico e Cultural de Macao, 2011

Iaccarino, Ubaldo, *"Manila as an International Entrepôt: Chinese and Japanese trade with the Spanish Philippines at the close of the 16th century"*, Naples: L'Università degli Studi di Napoli L'Orientale, BPJS 2008, 16, pp.71-81; on-line at www.redalyc.org

de Morga, Antonio , *Sucesos de las islas Filipinas* [1609], ed. W.E.Retana, Madrid: 1909

de Morga, Antonio, *Sucesos de las Islas Filipinas*, tr. J. S. Cummins, (Hakluyt Society), Cambridge: Cambridge University Press, 1971

" Memoria de las Encomiendas en las Islas" [1591] in *The Philippine Islands,* vol.6

The Philippine Islands, 1493-1803 ed. Emma Helen Blair et al; on-line at www.gutenberg.net – numerous texts on the history of the Philippines

The Japanese in the Philippines

The exact date for the beginning of relations between Japan and the islands that now make up the Philippines is debated, but casual contact probably occurred throughout the Middle Ages, as the Japanese were interested in acquiring local products. Favourite items were deer skins – in the 1580s they had a settlement in the Pangadinan district specifically for the purpose of collecting them, indeed they were so successful that in 1598 the Spanish banned the trade for fear the deer should become extinct – and the Luzon jars, dating from the Tang and Sung, described Antonio de Morga, which were very highly prized in Japan.

According to a report made to Miguel López de Legaspi, five years after the Philippines had been claimed for the crown of Spain, there were 20 Japanese living in Manila. By 1593, there were some 300-400 living in the Dilao quarter and this had risen to some 3,000 in the early 1600s. It was to increase yet further as the persecution of the Christians in Japan became more intense – for example in 1614 the daimyo convert, Takeyama Ukon, led 300 Christian refugees to safety in Manila. As a result of this Christian diaspora, Japanese communities – as opposed to visiting merchants – settled across South East Asia: at Ayutthaya, Hoi An, Patani, Ligor and elsewhere, as well as at Manila, although over time they tended to vanish into the local population.

Although at this stage the Spanish were somewhat less concerned with rising Japanese numbers than they were with the influx of Chinese, relations were very uneven. The Japanese took part in the unsuccessful Tondo Conspiracy of 1587-8, which saw a strange coalition of local lords, a Japanese naval commander and the great-grandson of Legaspi confront the Spanish authorities.

In 1603, a Chinese embassy triggered fear of an invasion from the mainland. The Spanish, already outnumbered 20 to 1 by the Chinese and worried by mass immigration, when faced with an initially successful rebellion led by a trusted Chinese Catholic, instituted a massacre in which both locals and, especially, the Japanese community, took enthusiastic part. Some 20,000-30,000 Sangley, as pure-blooded Chinese were known in the Philippines, died. Mainland China showed little interest. Emigration was officially forbidden and the fate of those who had "turned their backs on the tombs of their ancestors" was felt to be of little importance. By 1605, trade relations had returned to normal.

Three years later, it was the Japanese' turn to rebel. According to de Morga, this was because "The *Audiencia* wished to drive a number of Japanese from this city, for they were a turbulent people and promised little security for the country." The Japanese resisted and de Morga continued: "This was one of the greatest dangers that had threatened Manila, for the Spanish were few in number, and the Japanese more than 1,500, and they are a spirited and very mettlesome race." De Morga's impression was perfectly correct: wherever the Japanese went – Manila, Macao, Mexico....they were immediately involved in brawls and the 19th c. *The Autobiography of a Tokugawa Samurai* gives a clear picture of the mindset that led to this turbulence. The uprising was eventually calmed, largely thanks to the influence of the Franciscan friars, who were in charge of the Christian Japanese community. The Japanese were again on the side of the Spaniards, repelling various attacks by the Dutch, during the 17th century.

Tokugawa Ieyasu was very anxious to enter into serious trade relations with Spain. In 1598, even before his power was consolidated at the Battle of Sekigahara, he had Fr. Geronimo de Jesús write a letter to try and persuade the Governor of the Philippines to allow the Mexican galleons to include Japan in their route, but the Spanish were reluctant for a variety of reasons. The ferocious protectionism of the Sevillian merchants certainly played a part, but there was also a distrust born of earlier threats of a Japanese invasion and again several occasions on which the Japanese had seized ships wrecked or grounded on their coast, for example the *San Felipe* in 1596 and the *Espiritu Santo* in 1602. In fact, it should hardly have seemed surprising: under ancient European maritime law, *ius littoris* or *ius naufragii* permitted this and Luís de Velasco, the Viceroy of New Spain, had just granted the people along the Gulf of Mexico the right to appropriate all shipwrecked goods. Another reason for the lack of response to Hideyoshi's overtures was simply *accidie*.

In 1601, Ieyasu sent another mission with a wealthy Sakai merchant, Shinkiro. The then Governor expressed interest, but claimed he was too busy with the war in Siam to give the matter the attention it deserved. A similar message was sent the following year, but this time, it also touched on the problem of pirates. Ever more serious from the mid 14th century, the depredations of Japanese pirates, *wakō* – although many were in probability not Japanese – had caused a disastrous breach with China, resulting in Japanese merchants being forbidden access to its markets. This, of course, worsened the problem of smuggling and piracy and made it vital for Japan to acquire trading partners who could act as intermediaries, in particular importing silk to Japan and silver to China. The Spanish in the Philippines had also suffered from the *wakō*. In 1582, for example, the Governor sent a squadron to dislodge Japanese pirates who had built a fort at Cagayan in Northern Luzon as a base from which to harass shipping.

Ieyasu offered to hunt down the pirates in the islands of Japan and offered a simple solution to the Spanish problem, and to that of seditious or turbulent Japanese in their territory: "Execute all Japanese who in the Philippines violate your laws." The message was repeated in a letter sent in September 1602, in which he added: "....and if among the merchants who go to your country with my permission any fail to submit to your authority, let me know their names that in the future I may prevent their ships from setting sail." In the following month he wrote again, offering permits for eight Spanish ships to put in at any port in Japan "without fear".

Successive Governors of the Philippines were evasive, until Roderigo de Vivero took up the post in 1608. The principal Japanese merchants of Manila begged him to pursue the negotiations and when Will Adams reached Manila with a new round of letters and suggestions for an agreement, Vivero replied both to Hideyoshi, who had nominally abdicated, taking the title Ōgosho-sama, and to his son Hidetada, giving a positive response. Curiously enough, Vivero does not mention that he had been in contact with Hideyoshi before the shipwreck. Both Hideyoshi and Hidetada continued to stress the rigour of the Japanese legal system "as a result of which, we have neither thieves nor miscreants", and in the following year, to reassure Vivero's successor, Juan de Silva, who was unenthusiastic about the Japanese: "a turbulent people much given to fighting", they sent a copy of the Japanese law code, suggesting that he apply it to any trouble makers.

Vivero's shipwreck on the way home provided an excellent opportunity for Ieyasu to consolidate mercantile relations with Spain which was, of course, what really interested him, as well as negotiating for mining technicians from New Spain to advise on Sado and Izu. The brutal examples of Japanese justice that Vivero witnessed were no doubt intended to reassure the Spanish contingent that there were effective ways of dealing with miscreants – and perhaps also to act as a warning. It is somewhat surprising that a military man from 17th century Mexico should have been shocked by them.

Bibliography

Iaccarino, Ubaldo, "*Manila as an International Entrepôt: Chinese and Japanese trade with the Spanish Philippines at the close of the 16ᵗʰ century*", Naples: L'Università degli Studi di Napoli L'Orientale, BPJS 2008, 16, pp.71-81; on-line at *www. redalyc.org*

Katsu, Kokichi, *Musui's Story – The Autobiography of a Tokugawa Samurai*, tr. Teruko Craig, Tucson: University of Arizona Press 1988

Morga, Antonio de, *Sucesos de las islas Filipinas* [1609], ed. W.E.Retana, Madrid: 1909

Verzijl, J.H.W., *International Law in Historical Perspective*, Leyden: Martinus Nijhoff, 1971

The Japanese in South East Asia

Vivero makes references to Japan's overseas contacts, for example the "two ambassadors whom the Emperor was sending to the kingdom of Siam" hung on the orders of André Pessoa in the unfortunate incident at Macao in 1608.

Everyone wanted to trade with China, but the Chinese authorities made it extremely difficult. In 1567, they had repealed their ban on South East Asian trade, but the laws forbidding Japanese merchants from entering China, and the Chinese from visiting Japan, were still in force. The Japanese were therefore forced to trade through third parties and various places in S.E.Asia served as neutral territory.

Hoi An (in modern Vietnam) was a popular choice, because of the favourable terms offered and the fact that there they did not have to deal with "barbarians", as at Manila. The Nguyen rulers encouraged foreign trade and were in correspondence with Tokugawa Ieyasu and his successors. There are still traces of the Japanese presence in Hoi An today.

Another favourite emporium was Ayutthaya in Siam (modern Thailand), at that date a flourishing and surprisingly international city. Substantial numbers of Japanese lived there – c.1500 in 1620 – in various capacities: mercenaries, merchants and Christians fleeing the persecutions at home. Fr. António Francisco Cardim, a Portuguese Jesuit, reportedly administered the sacrament to some 400 Japanese on a Feast Day in 1627[1].

The arms trade – both traditional Japanese weapons and ones of Portuguese origin – was of particular importance, since Siam was embroiled in wars with Burma, and Japan was very anxious to foster exports. Formal relations were initiated in 1606 and six embassies from Siam visited Japan between 1616 and 1629.

[1] Cited in Antonio Gomes, *Summario de Bibliotheca Lusitana*, Lisboa, 1786, vol.I, p.131.

Bibliography

Breazeale, Kennon ed. *From Japan to Arabia: Ayutthaya's maritime relations with Asia*, Bangkok, 1999, especially Nagazumi, Yoko, "Ayutthaya and Japan: Embassies and Trade in the Seventeenth Century"

Denison, Donald ed. *Multicultural Japan, Cambridge University Press, 1996,* especially, Ishii Yoneo, "Siam and Japan in pre-modern times: a note on mutual images"

Iwao, Seiichi, "Japanese Foreign Trade in the 16th and 17th centuries" in *Studies in the History of Foreign Trade in Early Modern Japan*, Acta Asiatica vol 30, Tokyo, 1976

Keene, Donald, *The Battles of Coxinga: Chikamatsu's Puppet Play*, Cambridge University Press, 1971

Polenghi, Cesare, *Samurai of Ayutthaya: Yamada Nagamasa, Japanese Warrior and Merchant in Early 17th Century Siam*, Bangkok, White Lotus, 2009

The Political Situation in Japan

Vivero arrived in Japan at a particularly significant moment, when the country was being unified and undergoing great changes, political and social. He was not in a position to have a clear understanding of events, and probably did not realise that the Shogun's priorities were unifying the country (incidentally putting an end to the chaos beautifully depicted in Kurosawa's *The Seven Samurai*, set in 1587), improving the economy – and, above all, retaining power. No foreigner or foreign demand was of comparable importance.

There are excellent books on the subject, so the following is a minimal outline to explain some of the points which Vivero leaves unclear.

Japan's dual system of an Emperor, who had come to be of largely ritual importance and often even impoverished, and a military government, the *bakufu*, headed by the Shogun, confused foreign visitors, and not only Vivero. They often referred to the Shogun as the "king", or thought he was the Emperor. An added cause of confusion was the custom of *insei*. This involved the abdication and withdrawal, usually to a monastery, of the older sovereign in favour of his heir, while retaining important advisory powers. It was largely a phenomenon of the Heian Period, but continued in a modified form until the 18th century. Furthermore, the first Tokugawa Shoguns followed the imperial pattern, with Ieyasu, abdicating in 1605 in favour of his third son, Tokugawa Hidetada, although as *Ogosho* – Retired Shogun – he retained the real power. Vivero was, understandably, somewhat perplexed.

The Ashikaga shogunate, which ruled from 1338-1573, was comparatively weak and the Onin War of 1467-77, which was a dynastic dispute, left the capital, Kyoto, in ruins.[1] Subsequently, fighting among the increasingly powerful independent daimyos, or warlords, escalated and the country descended into a state of instability and conflict known as *Sengoku-jidai*, or Warring States –

a term borrowed from the Chinese. This situation again confused foreigners, who often refer to the daimyos as kings, which in effect many of them were by the time Europeans first reached Japan in the mid-16th century.

Among the daimyos struggling for power, Oda Nobunaga was the first of the three great unifiers, followed by Toyotomi Hideyoshi and Tokugawa Ieyasu. Around the time of Vivero's journey, Japan had moved from a country involved in a devastating multidirectional civil war, with very limited external contacts, to a unified nation, avid for trade and new forms of learning, having experienced a new religion, with embassies sent to Europe, the Philippines and Mexico, and with settlements in the countries that are now Thailand, Malaysia and Vietnam, as well as their own quarter in Manila.

Before Vivero had actually written up his voyage, however, everything had changed yet again and in 1639, three years after his death, the period of openness was over. For a complex series of reasons – among them, an increasing sense that Christianity was incompatible with the Japanese traditional ethos, fear of Spain's military intentions, concern that the Christian daimyos were plotting against the state, disgust at the Portuguese enslaving Japanese nationals, disillusionment brought on by the disagreements and backbiting among the different European communities, the failure of trade opportunities and technological expectations – the Shogun decided that the foreigners were more trouble than they were worth and Japan would do better without external contacts and interference. The period of *sakoku* – the chained country – had begun and Japan was to have only the most minimal contact with the outside world for some 250 years.

[1] Now the city that you know
     Has become an empty field,
     From which the skylark rises
     And your tears fall...
                    From the Onin Ki cited on Wikipedia under "Onin Wars"

Bibliography

Gordon, Andrew, *A Modern History of Japan: from Tokugawa times to the present*, Oxford University Press, 2009

Najita, Tetsuo, ed., *Tokugawa Political Writings*, Cambridge University Press, 1998

Pratt, Peter, *History of Japan, compiled from the Records of the East India Company (1822)*, London and New York, 1972

Sansom, George, *A History of Japan*, London, 1978

The Cambridge History of Japan vol IV, Cambridge University Press, 1991

Watanabe, Hiroshi, *A History of Japanese Political Thought 1600-1901*, tr. David Noble, Tokyo, 2012

The Introduction of Firearms into Japan

A crude type of cannon of Chinese origin – *teppō* – was known in Japan as early as the 13th century. The first recorded European firearms reached the country with Portuguese traders who arrived at Tanegashima, south of Kyushu, on a Chinese junk in 1543 or 4, only five years before St Francis Xavier landed at nearby Kagoshima on August 15th, 1549.

The junk carrying the merchants was damaged and in need of repair and, during their stay, the lord of the island, Tanegashima Tokitaka, came to hear of the Portuguese muskets and acquired a couple of them. Seeing great possibilities, military and commercial, he had one of the islands top sword-smiths, Yaita, attempt to copy them. According to a romantic story, probably a later legend, Yaita's daughter, Wakasa, was given in marriage to one of the Portuguese in exchange for certain production secrets.

Fernão Mendes Pinto describes the introduction of arquebuses, known in Japanese as *tanegashima teppō* from the name of the island, although he was almost certainly not among the first arrivals as he claimed. Muskets were soon in use throughout the country and were manufactured at Tanegashima, which had a good source of iron, and elsewhere, especially Sakai. The Portuguese also taught the people of Tanegashima the art of making gunpowder – charcoal and sulphur were available locally, indeed sulphur and swords were major exports to China, but saltpetre had to be imported, from China or Siam (modern Thailand). All this was an important stimulus to trade, since arms of every kind were in great demand and muskets played a prominent part in the ceaseless wars of the Sengoku period.

Initially slow and cumbersome, the Japanese made a number of technical and design improvements to the firearms, which radically changed military tactics. Hideyoshi and Nobunaga's battle at Nagashino in 1575 was the first military engagement in which systematic use was made of "modern" weaponry with some 3,000 arquebuses in the field, and a quarter of the invasion force of Korea in 1592 were gunners, explaining, to some extent, the extraordinary speed of conquest. Firearms were to have considerable social, as well as military impact, since they potentially democratised warfare, previously the prerogative of the highly trained samurai elite. The Japanese chronicle *Teppō-ki* or *History of the Arquebus* (c.1598-1640) describes the impression made by the foreigners and their firearms.

Bibliography

Brown, Delmer M. "The Impact of Firearms on Japanese Warfare, 1543-1598", *The Far Eastern Quarterly* May 1948 (Volume 7, Number 3: pp. 236–253), Association for Asian Studies.

Lidin, Olof G., *Tanegashima: the arrival of Europe in Japan*, Copenhagen: NIAS, 2002

Nanpo Bunshi, *Teppō-ki*, c. 1604, tr. in Tsunoda, et al., *Sources of Japanese Tradition*, New York: Columbia University Press,1958, pp. 308-312

Black Ships and Red Seals

China's reluctance to engage in foreign trade probably contributed to the rise of piracy, especially from the mid-14th to the late 16th century. The immediate cause for the sudden escalation seems to have been action by the Emperor Hongwu of the Ming. Fearing that foreigners, and specifically the seaborne *wakō* (pirates), would conspire with disaffected elements to reinstate the Mongol (Yuan) dynasty, in 1374 he effectively abolished such legitimate international trade opportunities as existed. This meant a return to the traditional "tribute missions".

Although the *wakō* were generally considered Japanese, they were in fact gangs of mixed origin, but frequently Kyushu-based and under Japanese leadership. They had a disastrous impact on the coastal areas of East Asia, leading to a number of strategies to circumvent them, and were one of the reasons the Japanese were forbidden access to China. The Chinese themselves did surprisingly little to control the *wakō*, although the great admiral Zheng He made a brief attempt.

From the end of the 14th century, the Koreans, on the other hand, developed an intelligent and effective strategy for dealing with the pirates, allowing them to trade and even settle. (A similar pattern was adopted with the Vikings in certain areas of Europe, also with some success). After centuries during which there had been had very little control, the Tokugawa Shogunate was anxious to exert their power on sea as well as on land, and exhorted the governors of the Philippines to execute pirates whenever they found them. By the 16th century, pressure from all directions was bringing the situation under control and Fr.Matteo Ricci, writing in 1584, describes the *wakō* as being a problem, although much less than they had been, and ten years later Fr.Valignano considered that they were no longer a major issue.

In theory, the only exception to the ban on trade with China were so-called tribute missions, which the Japanese (and other foreigners) used to disguise trading opportunities, while the Chinese chose to think of them as embassies from "barbarian nations" bearing tribute and offering submission to the Son of Heaven. At a certain point, as more and more merchants tried to disguise their trading ventures as embassies, these missions became too much of a burden – since traditionally all their expenses in the country were born by the Chinese government – and efforts were made to limit them.

The Japanese – like Tamerlane in Central Asia at the same date – violently objected to being considered "tributaries" with its explicit connotation of vassalage. This never involved military domination, however, or even serious interference with government, apart from symbolic requests such as the adoption of the Chinese calendar. When the Ashikaga Shogun Yoshimitsu offered submission to China in exchange for trade advantages and was given the title of *Nippon Koku-Ō*, or King of Japan, there was considerable outrage, expressed also by his son.

Relations continued to deteriorate, although both sides were eager for the other's products. Japan had an enormous appetite for Chinese silk and similar luxuries, especially as the country became increasingly peaceful and prosperous under the Shogunate, while they exported weapons – one ship was recorded as carrying 9,500 swords – silver and miscellaneous art works, including in the same shipment 630 scroll paintings, making clear that Japan was a civilised not a barbarian country, with desirable cultural artefacts, not simply raw materials.

A letter dated 1401, cited in *Ashikaga Yoshimitsu's Foreign Policy – Zenrin Kokuhōki* lists what were clearly presents rather than simply trade items, although the gold would have been expected to bring handsome "return gifts". It states:

"....we are sending...to establish friendly relations and to offer native products...one thousand ounces of gold, ten horses, one thousand packets of fine paper, three pairs of folding screens, one suit of armor, one breast plate, ten swords, one short sword, one ink slab with box, and one writing desk...." [1]

Another letter mentions 10,000 lbs of sulphur, used in gunpowder, fireworks and medicine.

The organisation of the genuine diplomatic missions and sanctioned commerce was traditionally in the hands of the Zen priesthood, as the best educated men in Japan. As early as 1342, two trading ships had gone to China and the profits used to build the Tenryū-ji, the Zen temple of the outskirts of Kyoto. More ships followed and as a result were often known as *Tenryūjibune* – Tenryū-ji ships. Trade between China and the temple, rather than the secular powers, allowed mercantile exchanges, without raising the diplomatic issue of Japan being a vassal of China. Instead, China controlled the appointment of the abbot of Tenryū-ji. The arrangement did not please everyone: "...the matter of our two countries' friendly relations should not be decided by Zen monks...." complains the *Zenrin Kokuhōki* [2].

As a result of this, there was nothing strange for the Japanese in priests engaging in major international trading ventures, and the Jesuits followed the tradition which allowed the Japanese access to much sought-after luxury goods without either having to place themselves in a humiliating posture vis-à-vis China, or deal with the *wakō*. The Jesuit/Portuguese connection at Macao was a distinctly preferable way of circumventing the Chinese ban on direct trade.

By the 17th century, ships were licensed by the Bakufu to carry on official overseas trade. They were known as *Go-shuin-sen* or Red Seal Ships because of the red seals on their *shuin-jō*, or sea passports. Certain years Europeans, including Will Adams, were granted permits and made up as many as a sixth of those to whom licenses were issued. In the early part of the century, until Japanese shipbuilding and navigational techniques improved, the Red Seal Ships were supposed to have a Portuguese pilot on board and they are to be seen in certain contemporary paintings, notably the votive pictures preserved at Kiyomizudera in Kyoto. A number of Portuguese-Japanese portulans survive from this period, as further evidence of the close cooperation – too close, according to some. Fr Valentin de Carvalho complained bitterly that Portuguese pilots would "for good pay" transfer knowledge and advantage to the Japanese.

Again because of the *wakō* and the desire of the Japanese for Chinese luxury goods, the annual trade ship from Macao, where the Portuguese had had trading privileges since 1557, gained great political importance as a bargaining point. The ship, sent once a year, was known in Portuguese as *nao do trato*, and in Japanese as *kurofune*, or black ship, because of its colour. The ships are shown on a number of the famous Japanese screens, known as *Namban-byōbu* – southern barbarian screens – because of their genre scenes of foreign life. The ships were very large carracks of up to 1600 tons and the cargo would consist almost entirely of luxuries and bullion, worth a million gold pesos or more. Too big to be much troubled by the *wakō*, they were to become the prime target of Dutch pirates when they entered Chinese and Japanese waters towards the end of the 16th century.

Several daimyo tried to attract the *kurofune* to their shores, because of the profit it would generate, but also to some extent for the prestige. The Jesuits were very anxious that it should dock in the harbour of a Christian daimyo so as to increase their influence, while the ships' captains were much more interested in finding a safe port and a good market. In 1571, the *kurofune* came for the first time to Nagasaki, which had a splendid harbour, and the local daimyo, Ōmura Sumitada, whose baptismal name was Don Bartolomeu, gave land to the Jesuits on which an essentially Christian community grew up.

From this point on, the *kurofune* became increasingly vital to the Jesuits, both economically – many of their converts were poor – and as the main reason that the Edict of Banishment was not implemented: successive rulers feared that evicting the Jesuits would lead to loss of the *kurofune*. In fact, that would probably not have been the case. After the martyrdoms of 1597, Valignano tried desperately to have the sailing of the *kurofune* cancelled, as the most effective form of pressure – but in vain. There were also, intermittently, plans to introduce a Spanish answer to the Portuguese *kurofune* sailing from Manila rather than Macao. This was an idea much encouraged by Vivero, but it never came to fruition, largely because of protests from Portuguese. The Manila trade was therefore carried on through the Red Seal ships.

Among the remarkably varied books printed in Japan by the Jesuits in the years 1590-1614, it would be of great interest to have one of which – so far – only the title has survived: *Kurofune Monogatari* – The Tale of the Black Ship.

[1] p.286
[2] p.284

Bibliography

Boxer, C.R., *The great ship from Amacon: annals from Macao and the old Japan trade –*
1555-1640, Lisboa: Centro de Estudos Históricos ultramarinos, 1959

Schurz, William Lytle, *The Manila galleon*, New York: Dutton, c.1939

Stone, Caroline, *"The Diplomacy of the Sons"*, Saudi Aramco World, May-June,
2006, on-line at *www.saudiaramcoworld.com*

von Verschuer, Charlotte, *"Ashikaga Yoshimitsu's Foreign Policy 1398 to 1508 A.D.:*
A Translation of the Zenrin Kokuhōki, the Cambridge Manuscript", Tokyo: Sophia
University, Monumenta Nipponica vol.62, No.3, Autumn 2007, pp.261-297

Yamafune, Kotaru, *Portuguese Ships on Namban Screens*, on-line at:
japanesembassies. files. wordpress.com/2013/01/yamafune-thesis.pdf

Japan and Korea – 1592-1598

Vivero makes a number of mentions of Japan's invasion of Korea, naturally from the Japanese standpoint – it is interesting to see the version that he was given – so it is perhaps worth summarizing events which still cast a shadow on international relations today.

The coasts of China and Korea – and sometimes also Japan – suffered from serious and repeated raids by the pirates known as *wakō*. There is disagreement as to their origins, but in the 16th-17th centuries they were generally considered to be Japanese, although they were in fact outlaws from a range of ethnic groups. This caused severe tensions between Korea and China, which perceived itself as Korea's overlord and protector, and Japan. Ill feeling was heightened by Japan's absolute refusal to accept China's overlordship and an inferior position as a "tribute-paying nation".

As far back as the time of Oda Nobunaga, there had been plans for an invasion of China, perhaps with the ancillary aim of getting rival war-lords out of the country, but Hideyoshi seems to have thought more in terms of Japan's smaller neighbours Taiwan and Korea, and to give himself legitimacy through military conquest; the result were the Imjin Wars.

The invasion was launched in 1592. Vivero's figures are, if anything, an underestimate: 158,000 men took part in the first wave with some quarter of a million being involved in the course of the war. Because of the *wakō*, Korea had developed a powerful navy but, in spite of repeated raids by the Jurchen tribes, which were at this date uniting to become the Manchu, their army was no match for the Japanese soldiery hardened by almost constant internecine wars. Again, because of their contact with the Portuguese, the Japanese had much more up-to-date firearms; aware of their naval weakness, they had also tried to hire Portuguese galleons.

The initial attack and advance took place at great speed and at first looked like a decisive victory, although repeated naval defeats, especially by Admiral Yi and his heavily armed "turtle ships", led to serious supply problems. It was this, as well as the Ming threat of sending in 400,000 men to support the Koreans, that led the Japanese to withdraw in 1593. A Chinese delegation came to Japan and a truce was negotiated which lasted from 1594-6 with Hideyoshi suggesting that they should divide Korea: China taking the North and Japan the South.

In 1597, hostilities began again, largely because Hideyoshi broke the terms of the truce and on the 5th of July he wrote in a private letter to his wife:

> "I have sent fast ships in order to urge even Korea to do homage to the Emperor of Japan, stating that, if it does not, I shall conquer it next year. I shall take even China in hand and have control of it during my lifetime; since [China] has become disdainful [of Japan], the work will be the more exhausting..."[1]

In another letter, he promised his mother, Ō-Mandokoro, that she would celebrate "the festival of the 9th month in the capital of China".

Meanwhile, with remarkable speed, Korea had been analyzing the reasons for its defeat and doing everything possible to remedy the situation, improving defenses and training males at all levels of society to bear arms. The second invasion of Korea – this time China was not included in the battle plan – proved much more difficult than the first and soon the Japanese found themselves on the defensive. On September 18th, 1598, Hideyoshi, on his deathbed, ordered the withdrawal from Korea. He is alleged to have said: "Do not let my soldiers become spirits in a strange land."[2]

Captives brought to Japan from Korea – 60,000 is probably an underestimate – had enormous influence on Japanese arts, as well as medicine and technology; conversely, their enslavement did great damage to Korea through loss of skilled manpower. Women of course were brought as well as men and forced, as in a later century, to serve as "comfort women". The Jesuit chroniclers mention the outstanding courage of the Korean martyrs, especially the women, during the persecutions.

Something more sinister to modern sensibilities was brought from Korea. The Japanese shared the custom, common across the Central Asian steppes, of collecting heads as proof of efficacy in battle. Because Korea was far from Japan, the severed heads were lined up for a traditional post-battle viewing and then mutilated, as described by the monk Keinen in his dispassionate account of atrocities against the civilian population:

"During a period of ten days, we seized 10,000 of the enemy, but we did not cut off their heads. We cut off their noses, which told us how many heads there were..."[3]

On Hideyoshi's orders, the noses were sent to Japan and some 38,000 of them were buried in a mound by the Toyokuni Jinja built to honour him. Vivero visited and admired Taikosama's tomb, but clearly was not shown what is now known as Mimizuka or "Hill of Ears", this being considered less brutal than the original name: Hanazuka or "Hill of Noses". The return of these remains an on-going diplomatic issue between Japan and Korea. In 1983, however, another mound with an estimated 20,000 noses was discovered at Okayama near Osaka and these were subsequently repatriated.

Tsushima was badly affected by the loss of trade with Korea and, in spite of the bitterness of the fighting, already in 1599 four peace missions had been dispatched. By 1603-4, after complex negotiations, a measure of normality had been re- established and by the time Vivero reached Japan, diplomatic and, to some extent, economic relations had been resumed.

[1] Boscoro p.31
[2] Turnbull, p.197
[3] Keinen's very remarkable diary, the *Chosen Nichinichiki*, is cited in James B.Lewis *The East Asian War, 1592-1596: International Relations, Violence and Memory*, p.85.
See also George Elison, "The Priest Keinen and His Account of the Campaign in Korea, 1597-1598: An Introduction" in the *Cambridge History of Japan*, vol.4, p.292.

Bibliography

Berry, Mary Elizabeth, *Hideyoshi*, Cambridge, Mass: Harvard University Press, 1982

Boscaro, Adriana, *101 Letters of Hideyoshi*, Tokyo: Sophia University, Monumenta Nipponica monographs, 54, 1975

Hawley, Samuel, *The Imjin War: Japan's Sixtenth-Century Invasion of Korea and Attempt to Conquer China*, Seoul: Royal Asiatic Society – Korea Branch, 2005

Kim, Ki-chung. "Resistance, Abduction, and Survival: The Documentary Literature of the Imjin War (1592–8)." *Korean Culture* 20:3 (Fall 1999), pp. 20–29

Turnbull, Stephen. *Samurai Invasion: Japan's Korean War 1592–98*. London: Cassell & Co, 2002

von Verschuer, Charlotte, "*Ashikaga Yoshimitsu's Foreign Policy 1398 to 1508 A.D.: A Translation of the Zenrin Kokuhōki, the Cambridge Manuscript*", Tokyo: Sophia University, Monumenta Nipponica vol.62, No.3, Autumn 2007, pp.261-297

The Other Side of the Coin: Admiral Yi

Although it is not strictly relevant to Vivero himself, it is impossible to resist giving some idea of the Korean campaign that he describes from the point of view of the great Korean Admiral Yi Sun-sin (1545-1598), who was to a large extent responsible for the ultimate defeat of the Japanese, not only at sea, but also by cutting their supply routes and preventing reinforcements from landing. Admiral Yi is famous for his strategy, often against far superior forces, and his design of the heavily armoured "Turtle Ship", completed just before the beginning of Hideyoshi's first invasion in 1592.

Admiral Yi's *Nanjung Ilgi* – or War Diary – begins in 1592. It is a remarkable mixture of stark description of naval and administrative procedures, and reports of weather conditions, mixed with intensely personal flashes of feeling. He speaks of his family, in particular his affection for his mother – although he was also deeply attached to his children and nephews and nieces, and other relatives and members of his household are mentioned with great affection. He recounts his dreams, and the occasional almost haiku-like description, for example, at night on his battle ship: "The moon shines in perfect beauty as if in an idealized painting.....the waves like silk brocade..."

Illness and depression feature largely, the latter caused in part by the intrigues against him at court, which led more than once to his being demoted. In 1597, he was even imprisoned, in spite of an unbroken run of victories against the Japanese. A picture builds up of the complexity of the social and political situation in Korea itself and, of course, the feelings towards the enemy. The following brief quotations from Ha Tae-hung's translation aim to show something of the other side of the coin described by Vivero.

The diary begins at the 5th moon of 1592 and almost immediately, on the 2nd day, news comes of officers who "hearing the news of the Japanese invasion fled immediately, weapons and war supplies scattered and lost – Terribly shocking!" On the 29th he was repelling the enemy advance and was wounded by an enemy bullet, but

"...countless heads of the enemy were cut off."p.5

A month later, he describes an attack on twenty Japanese vessels. On the deck of one of them "...stood a pavilion as high as two fathoms and, in the pavilion sat a Japanese commander in an exalted manner..." when

"...its commander fell, shot with an arrow, causing his frightened sailors to flee with wild shrieks..." p.6

On various other occasions, however, he comments on the complete impassivity with which Japanese prisoners faced death.

At the beginning of the 3rd moon in 1593, Admiral Yi was waiting anxiously for news of the Ming reinforcements, which were to prove unreliable and cause numerous problems, military and social. It should have been the spring festival – "Green Treading Day", but:

"The cruel Japanese enemy do not retreat and I have to float on the water with my sailors to drive them out. I have not yet heard that the Ming reinforcements have captured Seoul. Agony rests on my heart, rain falls on the sea all day." p.20

Shortly after, constant campaigning led to a gap in the diary between the 3rd and 4th moons:

"While I wish to keep all daily events in written record, due to my busy programs on land and sea with no time to rest, I have long forgotten to keep my diary (as I did forget sometimes in the past). From here I must continue writing once again." pp.23-4

He spent the New Year of 1594 at home with his mother and family, and was deeply upset at having to leave her looking so old and ill. Like Hideyoshi, he dreaded going grey, but in Admiral Yi's case it was for fear of worrying his mother rather than repelling his women. On the 12th, he had to return to his command:

"...I bid farewell to my mother. She said to me in a warm gentle voice, "Fight gallantly and wipe out the national disgrace." She repeated the same words to me. I had no other desire but what she taught me. She spoke this fond farewell without shedding tears or showing emotion..." pp.62-3

Admiral Yi was much troubled by the unreliability both of certain colleagues and the Ming forces, as well as the difficulty in knowing the truth of reports obtained both from Japanese defectors and Korean spies. Of one Commander who received a most savage royal reprimand for negotiating disloyally with the Japanese, he exclaimed:

"As yet I have not heard that he has repented and changed his mind. Had he had a bit of conscience he would disembowel himself to apologise for his guilt". (7th of the 7th moon, 1595) p.165

On the 9th and 10th of the 5th moon, 1594 he wrote:

"Rain. I sat alone in the empty pavilion, hundreds of thoughts ran to my mind, reminiscences perplexed my heart. It was beyond my expression. Muddled with dreamy thoughts I felt myself stupid, even crazy.

"Rain. At dawn I rose from my bed and opened the lattice wide, when all at once I saw a forest of our ships' masts covering the sea far over the horizon; if the enemy attack there is no doubt we can destroy them…" pp.90-1

He suffered frequently from insomnia, particularly apparently when the moon was full, and was occasionally soothed by listening to the playing of a flute.

Whenever possible, Admiral Yi, practised archery and there are a number of references to commissioning and making bows and arrows but, surprisingly, given his innovative battleship design, he never seems to have handled firearms, although they are often mentioned and he suffered a bullet wound early in the campaign. Later on the 23rd of the 6th moon, 1594 he writes:

"A Japanese prisoner was brought back to my camp and interrogated on the enemy positions and situation. When asked of his capabilities, he replied he was skilled in the production of gun-powder and the shooting of guns." p.99

Considerable numbers of the Japanese invading force were artillery-men. Other Japanese, who had surrendered, were set to work practising their particular crafts for example in construction (on the 13th of the 10th moon, 1595).

And there are other almost domestic details, for example on the 12th of the 10th moon of 1594:

"....the Field Marshal forwarded some winter-proof ear-muffs made of rat-skins to each naval station – 15 pairs to the Left Naval Station, 10 pairs to the right...." p.126

The New Year of 1595 was no happier than the previous one: 1st of the 1st moon, 1595

"Clear. Sitting alone under a lighted candle, I thought of the present state of the national affairs. I found tears rolling down my cheeks. Turning my heart toward my eighty-year-old mother in feeble health, I was disquieted the whole night." p.135

On the 11th of the 3rd moon, 1595 he received the following opinion from a colleague:

"....judging from the enemy strength in the Kyŏngsang Province, and the reports of the surrendered Japanese, it is clear that Hideyoshi has resolved to send more reinforcements across the sea in order to build permanent forts and barracks in Pusan. After seeing the lack of results in the three years of war in Korea. It is also said that he fixed the date for his convoy to cross the sea as the 11th of the 3rd moon." p.144

The issue of obtaining food supplies is mentioned frequently: bulk purchases of rice and herrings, making bean paste balls, drying seaweed and other staples. There are also fairly frequent drinking parties and occasionally, as on the 8th of the 1st moon of 1596:

"I invited.....in the morning to eat rice cake (cooked and flavoured with honey, sesame oil, dates and chestnuts) together." p.193

Early in the morning five surrendered Japanese entered the camp. On being questioned about the reasons for their escape, they explained that their commanding officer was a cruel fellow, driving them too hard, so they ran away and surrendered. The large and small swords in their possession were collected and put away in the attic of the pavilion..." p.193

On the 19th of the 4th moon:

"Early in the morning I heard of Hideyoshi's death through Minami Uyemon, and my joy knew no bounds, but the news was unreliable. There had been such a rumour going around although no definite information had been received." p.217

And on the 13th of the following month, he received a letter with the information that:

"...Kiyomasa (Kato) has already crossed the sea for home on the 10th, leading his army on transports. The Japanese commanders stationed in other positions will also evacuate. The Japanese in Pusan still remain there to escort the Ming Chinese envoy to their country..." p.222

Somewhat later, he mentions buying Japanese guns and on the 13th of the 7th moon, in a very different mode:

"After dark the surrendered Japanese played a drama with the make-up of actors and actresses. As Commanding Admiral, I could not attend, but since the submissive captives wished to entertain themselves with their native farce for enjoyment of the day, I did not forbid it." p.233

It would be very interesting to know what the Japanese were performing: a real play? Or an improvisation? Kabuki is first mentioned in 1603 – originally performed only by women; it was deeply disapproved of by the warrior class. Noh already existed and Hideyoshi not only had a passion for it, but was very proud of his mastery of a number of roles. Perhaps the most likely is some version of *kyogen*, since Admiral Yi may have meant "farce" literally, rather than as a term of disparagement.

On the 10th of the 8th moon, rather surprisingly, he invited several colleagues "..to make ornamental paper flowers to share together..." p.239

Later in the following month – a leap month – he was cheered at being able to visit his mother but his emotions were mixed and as he travelled back:

"En route my eyes witnessed the desolation in the country houses and farms, the misery which could not be borne in mind. Then, I thought I should first relieve the burden of the anxious sailors and the poor local inhabitants by exempting them from maintaining warships."p.245

The final entry in the *Nanjung Ilgi* was written on December 16th, 1598, the eve of his death, pursuing the retreating Japanese. His last words to his son and nephew are recorded as being: "Do not weep, do not announce my death. Beat the drum, blow the trumpet, wave the flag for advance. We are still fighting. Finish the enemy to the last one." Introduction, p.xxx

Bibliography

Strauss, Barry. "Korea's Legendary General", *MHQ: The Quarterly Journal of Military History* Summer 2005 (Volume 17, Number 4: pp. 52–61).

Yi, Sun-sin, *Nanjung ilgi – War Diary of the Admiral Yi Sun-sin* [1592-3 and 1594-6], tr. Ha Tae Hung, ed. Sohn Pow-key, Seoul: Yansei University Press, 1977

Silver and Silver Mines

The dream of the Conquistadores was to find gold, but in fact it was the silver mines of the New World that generated greater riches and had a more profound effect on the world economy. Between 1550 and 1800 an estimated 80% of the world's production came from Latin America – an estimated 136,000 metric tons. Much of this found its way into the financial systems of China and the Ottoman Empire.

The Romans were aware of the affinity of gold and silver for mercury, as were the Arabs. In the mid-16th century, a Sevillian merchant, Bartolomé de Medina, inspired perhaps by both his own and his country's economic problems, became interested in how silver could be produced more cheaply and efficiently than by the traditional smelting. Above all, there was the question of how lower grade ore and the residue left from previous extractions could be processed. He seems to have experimented in Seville, using the technique of mercury amalgamation, with the help of a German colleague of whom little is known, "El Maestro Lorenzo". His co-national, Georg Agricola was to describe the amalgamation process in his work *De re metallica* (1556).

The experiments were satisfactory, but getting the necessary materials was made difficult in Seville so, in 1553, Medina applied for passports for himself and Maestro Lorenzo for the New World. He was granted permission to leave but, in spite of repeated pleas to the authorities, Maestro Lorenzo, being a foreigner, was refused. Medina settled down in the town of Pachuca to continue his experiments and in 1555, he was able to write to the Viceroy of New Spain, Luís de Velasco, announcing his success with the so-called "patio process" – on account of the large amount of space required – and requesting a patent. A limited one was granted but, typically, Medina could not collect the royalties due to him and was never properly rewarded for his endeavours. He lost everything in a shipwreck returning to Seville in 1563 to appeal – fruitlessly – to the king. Thus, a refined version of the amalgamation process was first used on an industrial scale at the great silver mines in the New World. The process came at the ideal moment, since vast deposits had recently been discovered, especially Zacatecas in Central Mexico (1546) and Potosí in Bolivia (1546).

"If there were not mercury, nor would there be silver", said Luís de Velasco and in 1648 a later Viceroy added that Huancavalica and Potosí were "the two pillars that support this kingdom and that of Spain." Mercury, of course, was the key to the amalgamation process and the largest mines in the world, in use since antiquity, were at Almadén near Ciudad Real in Spain, closed since 2000 and named a World Heritage Site in 2012. During the 16th-17th centuries, these mines were administered by the German banking family, the Fuggers, to whom the Spanish Crown was deeply in debt. Most of the mercury was sent to Seville for export to the New World. In 1563-4, however, cinnabar mines were discovered at Huancavalica in Peru. This was a great advantage, for reasons of distance, but also because working in the mercury mines was so dangerous to health, as the Jesuit José de Acosta pointed out as early as 1590, that no-one would do it, except convicts – and even they preferred the galleys. In the New World, the Indians could be forced into the mines.

China had an insatiable appetite for silver and much of the bullion from the New World ended there. From the 16th century, the other great world producer was Japan. Originally, the Japanese had a relatively moderate interest in silver, although the Iwame Ginzan mine near Omori in Shimane Prefecture[1] had been in production since the early 16th century, and alluvial silver and gold had been found on Sado and elsewhere since at least the 8th c.

The arrival of the Portuguese in 1543 led to Japan joining the global monetary economy and the demand for precious metals for trade greatly increased. The unification of Japan and the end to the constant wars, also meant policies of economic development could be put in place and for these money, rather than the traditional rice, was required. The first mine – as opposed to collection by panning – on Sado had in fact opened in the previous year, and silver was present in the Kai, Idzu and Iwami regions. Five years later, anxious for funds to pay for his Korean campaign, it was seized by Hideyoshi, who sent mining experts to the island to speed up production.

Tokugawa Ieyasu similarly took a great interest in Sado and in 1600 the island was put under the direct control of the Shogunate and everything possible was done to stimulate operations. The discovery of the Aikawa mine, the most profitable on the island, greatly increased output, and gold was also found to be present on Sado. Until 1603, individual miners could bid for claims, but afterwards a more tightly controlled system was instituted to provide funding for long-term investment in such projects as tunnelling, draining, etc. Under the new system, roughly 40% went to the authorities and 60% to the mine operator, although these percentages varied over the years. Vivero's suggestion of a 50/50 split between the mine operator and the authorities would in fact have given the former a smaller percentage than in the standard Japanese contract, although of course the authorities, Japanese and Spanish, would have had to share the remainder.

Because of the importance of the mines, they were recorded not only through official documentation, but also visually with scrolls known as *kinginzan emaki* [illustrated scrolls of gold and silver mines] that showed all of the mining processes in great detail. They are hard to date, as they were frequently copied and, after the Meiji Restoration, were reproduced as a favourite gift to visitors with technical interests, but none are thought to be as early as Vivero's visit to Japan. An excellent article by Hamish Todd on the scrolls at the British Library can be found online at *www.bl.uk*.

[1] It became a World Heritage Site in 2007.

Bibliography

Lunde, Paul, *American Silver, Ottoman Decline*, SAW, May/June 1992 pp.34-7 and on-line at *www.saudiaramcoworld.com*

Menes Llaguno, Juan Manuel, *Bartolomé de Medina : un sevillano "pachuqueño"*, Pachuca : Universidad Autónoma del Estado de Hidalgo, 1989

Probert, Alan, *"The Patio Process and the Sixteenth Century Silver Crisis"* pp 96-127 in *Mines of Silver and Gold in the Americas*, ed.Peter Bakewell, Aldeshot: Variorum, 1997

Robins, Nicholas A. and Hagan, Nicole A., *"Mercury Production and Use in Colonial Andean Silver Production"*, Environmental Health Perspectives, May 2012, pp.627-631; on-line at *www.ncbi.nlm.gov*

Sasaki, Junosuke, *Modes of Traditional Mining Techniques*, IDE-JETRO, 1980, on-line at *www.d-arch.ide.go.jp*

Todd, H., *"The British Library's Sado Mining Scrolls – Kinginzanemaki"*, British Library Journal, 1998, vol.24, pp.130-143; on-line at *www.bl.uk*

The rise of merchant empires: long-distance trade in the early modern world, 1350-1750, ed. James D. Tracy, Cambridge : Cambridge University Press, 1990

Christianity in Japan and the Political Situation

The arrival of Christianity was not the first occasion on which Japan had found itself confronted with a new religion. Buddhism had been introduced in several waves from the 6th century – the Zen school not until the 12th – and by the time of Vivero it was very much more influential than the indigenous Shinto. It is probable, therefore, that the Japanese did not immediately comprehend the implications of a rigidly monotheistic religion that could not simply be added to pre-existing rituals and beliefs. The dissipating of the initial tolerance may in part have been connected with the growing realisation that Christianity was far more exclusive than Buddhism and would demand the eradication of earlier religious allegiances.

Japan's relationship with both Christianity and foreigners in general during the second half of the 16th century and early years of the 17th is complex and has generated a considerable literature in various languages. The following is an attempt to provide a very basic outline, in order to understand Vivero's remarks on the subject, but it should be born in mind that such a degree of simplification is, inevitably, inaccurate. The best and most accessible overview of the subject is still, after more than 60 years, C.R.Boxer, *The Christian Century in Japan*, while *The Southern Barbarians*, ed. Michael Cooper S.J. gives a different and interesting perspective, taking into account the cultural contacts among Japan, Europe and New Spain, and drawing on the voluminous Jesuit letters from Japan. Most of these last are, unfortunately, not easily available and, in the early printed editions, much descriptive material was excised by the Propaganda Fide as irrelevant – or unedifying – and statements such as this from a letter by the Italian Jesuit Fr. Organtino Gnecchi-Soldo written in the 1580s pleased no-one:

"You should not think they are barbarians, for apart from the Faith, however prudent we may think we are, we are great barbarians compared to them. In all truth, I confess that I learn from them every day, and I think there is no other nation in the world with so many talents and natural gifts as the Japanese."[1]

From the early 16th century, the Portuguese came across Japanese traders, or possibly *wakō*, the notorious pirates – in fact not necessarily Japanese – at Malacca and elsewhere. However, they seem not to have reached the southern islands of Japan until the 1540s. There is some debate as to who arrived first, but on August 15th, 1549, Francis Xavier of the recently founded Company of Jesus, later known as the Jesuits, landed at Kagoshima. His visit was at least partially inspired by a Japanese, Anjirō (later baptised at Goa as Pablo de Santa Fé), whom he met at Malacca and who assured him that Japan was a very promising field for missionary endeavour. Francis Xavier's letters show clearly that, like so many Europeans, including Vivero, he was enormously impressed by Japan and the Japanese, and was well aware that the approach to this very sophisticated culture would have to be quite different to the one he had been using among the pearl fishers of South India or in the Indonesian islands.

Educated and, on the whole, observant the Jesuits quickly realised that there would be no question of a military conquest of Japan. They were also aware that, while foreigners would be given a certain leeway – Fr Valignano writing about 1580 thought a couple of years – in which to learn something of the language and appropriate behaviour, if they persisted in flouting local norms (as did the British – Richard Cocks' diary makes this eloquently clear) they would be written off as unteachable savages. It was therefore a balancing act between adhering to Christian ethics[2] and being sufficiently flexible not to repel the nobility, on whom permission to remain, and hence make converts, ultimately depended.

Francis Xavier's start was difficult, in great part because he insisted on observing his vow of extreme poverty, but soon the Jesuits began to have a considerable success, both in Kyushu and in the area around Kyoto and Osaka. Although there were mixed feelings about the arrival of this new religion – the Emperors, as supporters of Buddhism (Shinto was at a very low ebb at this date), tended to be strongly opposed – nevertheless, as Anjirō had promised, there was considerable curiosity about the faith, but also about the culture, technology and mercantile opportunities that the Europeans represented. It is noteworthy that in the early years, in spite of the extreme instability of Japan and constant fighting during the *Sengoku* – or "Country at War" – period, no European Jesuit lost his life.

Oda Nobunaga (1534-82), the first of the three great unifiers of Japan, was extremely interested in European culture especially, but far from exclusively, firearms and trade. Although he did not convert to Christianity, he approved of the Jesuits, partly because he recognised that their discipline had something in common with *bushidō* and also because they shared a hatred of the Buddhist clergy – although his was based on political, rather than theological considerations. While they approved of it at the time (1571), Nobunaga's ruthless elimination of the Tendai warrior monks (*sōhei*) by burning the great monastery of Enryaku-ji at Hieizan outside Kyoto, leaving 3,000-4,000 dead, as punishment for their insubordination and support of the Emperor, might have offered the Jesuits a warning of the fate awaiting those who meddled in Japan's internal affairs.

Nobunaga allowed the Jesuits a fairly free rein, especially approving of their educational policies and he showed particular friendship to Fr. Luís Froís, who spoke excellent Japanese. Another minor, but curious, link was Yasuke, Fr Valignano's personal servant from Mozambique, who also spoke some Japanese. Nobunaga requested Yasuke for his own service and made him a samurai. Yasuke was present at the betrayal at Honnō-ji, where Nobunaga was treacherously attacked in 1582, and after Nobunaga's death, was returned to the Jesuits, who had been very concerned about his fate.

One seed of the eventual destruction of the Christian community in Japan was sown early. As far back as October 16th, 1578, Froís reports in a letter that it was widely believed that the Jesuits were waiting until they had enough converts to act as a Fifth Column, at which point they would summon an armada from India to add, in Boxer's phrase, "temporal to spiritual conquest." Nobunaga clearly paid no attention to these rumours, but they were to gain political force under subsequent rulers, in part because of the imprudent boasting, often naïf, as in the case of Vivero, of the power of the Spanish Crown and the extent of their conquests.

Nobunaga was succeeded by Toyotomi Hideyoshi (1536-98), the second of Japan's unifiers. A strange man, who had risen through the ranks to extreme power, his career was studded with sudden changes of policy and volte-faces. Initially, he was friendly to the Jesuits, especially Fr.Gaspar Coelho in part, like Nobunaga, through hatred of the Buddhist priesthood and awareness that the Jesuits were the portal whereby he could gain access to foreign trade goods. There was also the fact that, largely because of their precarious economic situation – *Socorro de España o llega tarde o nunca* (Help from Spain comes late or never) – they had very unwillingly been forced into the position of major bullion traders, as well as importers of silk through the "Great Ship" from Macao.

It has never been clear what happened on July 24th, 1587, the Vigil of the Feast of St James, when without warning Toyotomi Hideyoshi suddenly began questioning Fr. Coelho, confronting him with a series of accusations. On the following day, the Jesuits were banished as spies and traitors, and all Christian symbols proscribed. While it is true that Coelho had imprudently encouraged the destruction of Buddhist temples and images, and, like Vivero at a later date, had boasted of the conquests of the King of Spain and again – to Valignano's fury – had attempted some political manoeuvring among the Christian daimyos, there is no clear reason why the storm should have broken that night, although Valignano had pointed out in his *Sumario* of 1583 that the Japanese were never so fair spoken as when about to attack – Boxer invites a comparison with 1904 and 1941.

Equally – or perhaps more – mysterious is why the Edict of Banishment was never carried out. Perhaps Hideyoshi repented his fit of rage, or feared that it would put an end to the Macao trade. In any case, the Jesuits stayed, although much more discretely and with no further anti-Buddhist iconoclasm, and good relations were gradually resumed. Valignano was allowed to return in 1590 with the four young noblemen from Kyushu who had set out for Rome in 1583. In the following year, he was received by Hideyoshi – a tacit gesture of forgiveness, although the Edict was never repealed. He presented a range of rich and exotic gifts to Hideyoshi, who was to be seen strolling in the grounds of his palace wearing Portuguese dress and, as a fashion accessory, a rosary. Fr. João Rodrigues' linguistic skills – he had been in Japan since his early teens – furthered the Jesuit cause and brought him into considerable favour with Hideyoshi; indeed, he was with him on his deathbed.

In the early 1590s, the Jesuits finally lost their struggle, which involved complex political issues, including the question of Spanish and Portuguese spheres of influence, for the monopoly of the Japanese mission. The new-comers, especially the Franciscans, elected to ignore the battle plan drawn up by the Jesuits and forged ahead with the rough and ready strategies that had served them well in the Americas and the Philippines. They refused to accept that they were dealing with a vastly more sophisticated society, which could be won by the scholarship and learning of the Jesuits, by their art and music and the amazingly varied products of their printing press, but not by barefoot friars, who did not speak the language and associated with beggars and lepers; something Francis Xavier had discovered half a century before.

On October 19th, 1596, the *San Felipe* (the Spanish answer to the Portuguese *kurofune*), sailing from Manila to Acapulco, was wrecked on the Japanese coast and the cargo was seized by the local daimyo. This was protested by the Spanish Capitán Mayor who imprudently boasted of Spain's military might and stressed the role of the friars elsewhere in the world in opening the way for the conquistadores. On February 2nd of the following year, Hideyoshi had 26 Christians crucified at Nagasaki: four Spaniards, a Mexican, an Indo-Portuguese and 20 Japanese. The governor of the Philippines (which Hideyoshi had threatened to invade) wrote to protest and Boxer gives the reply as follows:

> "...and if, perchance, either religious or secular Japanese proceeded to your kingdoms and preached the law of Shinto therein, disquieting and disturbing the public peace and tranquility thereby, would you, as lord of the soil be pleased thereat? Certainly not; therefore by this you can judge what I have done..." [2]

The storm blew over, largely because Hideyoshi wanted trade to continue, as part of his policies for strengthening Japan and increasing its prosperity. He died in 1598 and the victor in the struggle for power, which culminated in the battle of Sekigahara in 1600, was Tokugawa Ieyasu (1542-1616), the third of the unifiers of Japan. Although he was a practising Buddhist, unlike his predecessors, Ieyasu was initially tolerant of the Christians and the faith spread rapidly in the first years of the 17th century. As a result, by 1606 the Jesuits could claim a community of 750,000 – although half this number is now generally felt to be a more plausible estimate – out of a population of c.18 million.

The situation for Christians, however, was less stable than it seemed and much less positive than Vivero imagined. Hideyoshi's priority was eliminating dissent and he was not prepared to tolerate it from the Christian daimyos. He was also not prepared to countenance visible in-fighting among different Christian groups, especially when this seemed likely to affect his plans for international trade by impeding the arrival of merchant shipping.

The situation worsened considerably with the arrival of the Englishman, Will Adams, in 1600. He quickly became a trusted advisor of Hideyoshi, supplanting Fr. Rodrigues and the Jesuits. Adams, English and Protestant, was no lover of the Spanish and Portuguese Catholics, although he and Vivero personally had a good relationship. He was, therefore, happy to tell Hideyoshi and his court of the divisions within Christendom, confirm their fears regarding the colonial ambitions of the Spanish and disabuse them of the notion that the Dutch were barbarous and piratical. In fact, Japanese experience was to confirm that this last was indeed the case, but by that time the country had closed to the outer world and their relationship with the Dutch was strictly on their own terms.

In 1609, Ieyasu's hostility to the Christians crystallised over the affair of the *Nossa Senhora de Graça*. It began in 1608, with a waterfront brawl in Macao, where some Japanese – who were forbidden to set foot on Chinese soil – found themselves stranded. The Chinese ordered the Portuguese to control the situation but, before they could arrange for their very unwelcome guests' departure, fighting broke out, with several killed on each side, including one Japanese apparently strangled in prison. Impossible to know at this date the rights and wrongs of the affair, but the Japanese had a bad reputation for brawling, wherever they went. André Pessoa, the Capitán Mayor, allowed the survivors to travel with him to Nagasaki, but ordered them to sign documents accepting the blame.

The ship succeeded in escaping Dutch pirates and, on arrival, Ieyasu at first gave credence to Pessoa's version of the event but, under pressure from various groups, changed his mind and commanded that the ship and its exceptionally rich cargo be seized. When Pessoa refused to give it up, Ieyasu gave orders that he should be taken dead or alive. Although warned, Pessoa, on board the *Nossa Senhora*, failed to escape, because of the lack of wind. He therefore prepared to fight and for three days held off hundreds of Japanese attackers. On January 6th, 1610, realising that the end was close and determined not to be taken alive, according to Fray Bernardino de Avila:

"Pessoa with intrepid heart put down his sword and shield in a cabin without saying a word and taking a crucifix in one hand and a firebrand in the other, went below and set fire to the powder magazine."[3]

The Japanese were deeply impressed by his suicide, which fitted perfectly with their ideas of honour. Ieyasu, however, was furious at being baulked of both revenge and booty – although attempts to retrieve the treasure from Nagasaki harbour have been made from 1610 until almost the present. Rodrigues was disgraced and forced to retire to Macao and the anti-Christian Edicts were revived and increasingly enforced. The maverick Fray Luìs Sotelo, relying on a powerful protector, Date Masamune, daimyo of Sendai, chose to flout them and built a small leper chapel at Asakusa. A number of Christians were put to death in reprisal; Sotelo himself was to die a martyr in 1624.

A reaction against Christian teaching also set in, with a number of anti-Christian works being produced such as the *Kirishitan Monogatari*. The subject is discussed and a number of texts are translated in George Elison's *Deus Destroyed*.

From 1614, the situation for the Christian population grew steadily worse. Ieyasu's son Hidetada (1579-1632), the second Shogun, was actively anti-Christian. He abdicated in 1623 in favour of his eldest son, Iemitsu (1604-1651). In complete contrast to the earlier rulers, they were also opposed to foreign trade, fearing that it would increase cultural contact with the outer world and be used as a cover for smuggling in priests. Under Hidetada, the Japanese, who had previously developed far-flung mercantile contacts, were forbidden to leave the country. Christians were forced to apostasize publicly, trampling under foot or otherwise desecrating their crucifixes and sacred images, and affiliating themselves officially with their choice of Buddhist temple. Those who refused were killed, often after appalling tortures. The Shimabara rebellion of 1637-8 confirmed the fears of the authorities and in 1640, the mass execution of an embassy from Macao, which came to plead for the Christian community, made Japan's position unequivocally clear.

The number of martyrs between 1614 and 1640 is thought to be 5,000-6,000. The authorities were enraged that peasants and "people of no account" should be so steadfast and that, bravest of all, were the Korean women slaves. There were, of course, numerous apostasies many, as the saying went, "from the teeth out". Christian Japanese also fled into exile, especially to places where there was a Catholic presence, of course Manila, but also Ayutthaya – the Jesuits recorded more than 400 there in 1626 – Annam, Tongking [Hanoi], Ligor and Patani, but some – *Kakure Kirishitan* (Hidden Christians) – went underground and kept the faith throughout the *Sakoku* period, only reemerging with the opening of Japan in the second half of the 19th century.

[1] *Southern Barbarians* p.137

[2] This issue was much debated. The Dominican Juan Paz wrote an *Opusculum*, published in Manila 1680 concerning "274 problems concerning which native practices could be permitted to converts in Tunkin [N.Vietnam]" and in India, the Jesuit Fr. Roberto de Nobili (1577-1656), actively, but controversially, insisted that customs not directly opposed to Christianity should be permitted to converts. He was supported by Pope Gregory XV, who nevertheless insisted that every effort should be made to fight against caste distinctions and the emargination of "outcasts".

[3] *Christian Century* p.161

[4] *Relación* p.125

Bibliography

Boxer, C.R., *The Christian Century in Japan, 1549-1650*, Berkeley, California: University of California Press, 1951

Cartas que os padres y Irmaõs da Companhia de Iesus escreverão das Reinos de Iapão y China....Evora: Manuel de Lyra, 1598

Cooper S.J., Michael, *The Southern Barbarians*, Tokyo: Kodansha/Sophia University, 1971

Cooper S.J. Michael, *The Japanese Mission to Europe, 1582–1590; The journey of Four Samurai Boys through Portugal, Spain and Italy*, Folkeston: Global Oriental, 2005

de Avila, Fray Bernardino, "Relación de Reino de Nippon", ch IV, pp.120-7, AIA [Archivo ibero-americano], año XXII, vol.38, Madrid, 1935

Elison, George, *Deus Destroyed: the Image of Christianity in Early Modern Japan*, Cambridge Mass.: Harvard University Press, 1973

Endō, Shusakū, *The Samurai*, tr. C. van Gessel, Tokyo: 1980

Exotic printing and the expansion of Europe, 1492-1840 (Exhibition catalogue) Bloomington, Indiana: Lilly Library, University of Indiana, 1972

Japanese Journal of Religious Studies – numerous articles available on-line at *www.nirc.nanzan-u.ac.jp* e.g.:

Kitagawa, Tomoko, "The Conversion of Hideyoshi's Daughter Gō", vol.34/1, Nagoya, 2007 pp.9-25

Midzunoe, Ikuko, "The Battle of the Books: Christian and Anti-Christian Tracts in the Early Seventeenth Century", Tokyo 2005 on-line at *www.pureb.cc.sophia.ac.jp*

Paz, Fr. Juan, *Opusculum*, Manila: 1608

Rodrigues João, *This island of Japon: João Rodrigues' account of 16th-century Japan.* [1610], tr. and ed. Michael Cooper, Tokyo: Kodansha International,1973

The Palme of Christian Fortitude. Or the glorious combats of Christians in Iaponia. Taken out of the letters of the Society of Jesus from thence. Anno 1624 tr. probably Edmund Sale S.J., Douai or St.Omer

Turnbull, Stephen, *The Kakure Kirishitan of Japan: A Study of Their Development, Beliefs and Rituals to the Present Day.* London: Routledge Curzon, 1998

Valignano, Alessandro, *Il Cerimoniale per i Missionari del Giappone,* [1581] ed. J.F.Schütte S.J., Rome: 1946

Valignano, Alessandro, *Sumario de las cosas de Japón, 1583,* ed. José Luìs Alvarez-Taladriz. Vol. 1, Tokyo : Sophia University, 1954

The Nuns of Kyoto

Vivero's description of his visit to the convent in Kyoto is of particular interest, although from the context, it was Buddhist, not, as might be expected, the sole Christian convent founded in Japan.

Although there were a number of confraternities and what were, essentially, associations of Tertiaries, the status of the one Christian convent was anomalous. The Jesuit Rule did not allow female foundations within the Order (those that were formed were unofficial and unrecognized) and Jesuit priests were enjoined to avoid acting as confessors to convents, except under exceptional circumstances.

The circumstances in Japan were certainly exceptional. For much of the "Christian Century", the Jesuits were the only Order in the country and they quickly realized that Japanese women would be immensely important in spreading the Christian message and that it was necessary both to interact with them and to provide them with the spiritual and intellectual support that they required. The principles enunciated by St Francis Xavier and implemented by such men as Fr.Alessandro Valignano concerning the need for cultural adaptation if the missionaries were to have maximum impact, led to their encouraging various forms of religious grouping among the women under their pastoral care.

Japanese women had good reason to be interested in the Christian message – quite apart from its emphasis on monogamy. Women had played an important role in Shinto, the indigenous religion of Japan, as priestesses and shamans, but by the latter part of the 16th century, Shinto was at a low ebb. Buddhism, in spite of reform movements such as Jōdō (Pure Land), relegated women to a position of insuperable inferiority and this was particularly true of Zen, much favoured by the dominant warrior class. Unless she could contrive to be reborn as a man, by her supreme virtue or through prayers – particularly those of her eldest son – the only afterlife awaiting a woman was eternal torment in the Lake of Blood, a favourite subject in numerous Hell Scrolls.

Nevertheless, many women craved and sought out a spiritual life and there were numerous convents and hermitages, as well as more informal lay associations. As in the West, Buddhist convents were also repositories for women who did not fit neatly into the social structure.

Buddhist nuns – *bikuni* – were not enclosed as were their European counterparts, particularly in the Hispanic world with its echoes of Islamic segregation and especially after the rigours of the Counter-Reformation. This made sense in the cultural context of Japan where the issue was ensuring legitimate offspring – obviously not relevant in the case of the *bikuni* – and there was no moral imperative to keep the sexes apart. Buddhist nuns were therefore free to go out and receive visitors, something which initially led to some misunderstandings by Europeans: Vivero would certainly not have expected such secular entertainment at a convent in Spain or in his native Mexico. It sounds, in fact, like a description of the ceremonial music and dance – *höe* – that was an intrinsic part of Buddhist ritual, especially on formal occasions

Fr. Luís Froís mentions this freedom in his *Tratado* of 1585 as one of the 68 differences between Japanese and Europeans. It was soon to change, however. Tokugawa Ieyasu, in his desire for control over every aspect of his subjects' lives, implemented a neo-Confucian ethic which soon eroded such freedoms as Japanese women had possessed.

The Christian message, which offered redemption to everyone regardless of sex and a readily comprehensible programme for washing away sin and reaching Paradise, clearly had great attractions and was surely one reason for the enthusiasm of the female converts. Another must have been the honour paid to the Virgin for having born Jesus, in sharp contrast to the idea of childbirth being expiated in the Lake of Blood.

The nuns of Kyoto – *Miyako no bikuni* – were established about 1600 by a most remarkable woman. Naitō Julia (her birth name is not known) had been, for a number of years, the abbess of a small Jōdō temple, and was highly regarded at the court of Hideyoshi for her learning and her eloquence. According to Fr. Luís Froís, her conversion in 1596 was rapid and spontaneous, triggered by a sermon that she heard given by a Japanese Jesuit, Irmão Hōin Vicente. She requested – and was probably granted – baptism in that same year. Her knowledge of Buddhist theology and skill in religious disputation was soon put at the Jesuits' disposal and there would have been considerable continuity for Naitō Julia between her life as Abbess of a temple and that as Mother Superior of a Christian religious community.

In 1605, a manual, the *Myōtei Mōndō*, was produced by another Japanese Jesuit, Irmão Fucan Fabian, for the use of women catechists, most probably with considerable input from the highly literate (eventually in European languages as well as Japanese) Naitō Julia and the other Sisters.

Ten years later, European nuns reached the Philippines: Velázquez painted his famous portrait of the formidable Abbess Jerónima de la Fuente, as she set out from Seville in 1619 to found the first official convent in the Far East. There is no evidence that any nuns ever reached Japan. However, intriguingly, they appear at least twice on the *namban byōbu* – "Southern barbarian screens" – in a Japanese context, their figures presumably copied from prints or paintings, wearing black and white habits.

In spite of the Edict of Banishment (1587), life for the Christians in Japan was fairly peaceful between 1600 and 1610, and numbers were growing, as Vivero describes. In 1612, however, Ieyasu moved to implement the Edict. Two years later, the church in Kyoto and the House of the *Bikuni* were destroyed. Naitō Julia hid the younger members of the congregation to protect them from rape or forced marriage, while the older women prepared for martyrdom. They were tortured for nine days, but none of them apostatized. It was then decided that they should be exiled and the Philippines offered them hospitality.

In February 1615, Naitō Julia and 14 other women, together with a number of European and Japanese Jesuits landed at Manila. The nuns – many of them of the high Japanese nobility – were welcomed and established in a convent near the capital. There the *Beatas*, as they were known, lived a cloistered life, perhaps in conformity with Hispanic custom, perhaps because, exhausted and disoriented by the experience of exile and its attendant linguistic and cultural problems, they no longer wished to move outside the small safe world of their convent.

[1] He later apostasized and wrote equally passionately against the Christian faith (see Elison)

Bibliography

Averbuch, Irit, *The Gods Come Dancing: A Study of the Japanese Ritual Dance of Yamabushi Kagura*, Ithaca, NY: East Asia Program, Cornell University, 1995, p. 15 [re bells in Shinto dance]

Elison, George, *Deus Destroyed: the Image of Christianity in Early Modern Japan*, Cambridge Mass.: Harvard University Press, 1973

Kitagawa, Tomoko, "The Conversion of Hideyoshi's Daughter Gō", Japanese Journal of Religious Studies, vol.34/1, Nagoya, 2007 pp.9-25, on-line at www.nirc.nanzan-u.ac.jp

Meeks, Lori, *Hokkeji and the reemergence of female monastic orders in premodern Japan*, Honolulu: University of Hawai'i Press, 2010

Ward, Haruko Nawata, *Women religious leaders in Japan's Christian century, 1549-1650*, Farnham, England: Ashgate, 2009

Slavery in Japan

One of the four major complaints made by Hideyoshi against the Portuguese, and hence the Christians, was that they were engaging in the slave trade. On July 24th, 1587, he wrote to the Jesuit vice-Provincial, Fr Gaspar Coelho:

> "....It has come to our attention that Portuguese, Siamese and Cambodians who come to our shores to trade are buying many people, ripping Japanese away from their homeland, families, children, and friends. This is insufferable. Thus, would the Padre ensure that all those Japanese who have up until now been sold in India and other distant places be returned again to Japan. If this is not possible, because they are away in remote kingdoms, then at least have the Portuguese set free the people whom they have bought recently. I will provide the money necessary to do this."[1]

The Jesuits were well aware of the problem. More than 30 years earlier, in 1555, they had complained to the authorities about the trade in Japanese girls whom they feared were being used for immoral purposes, while in 1571, King Sebastian of Portugal banned slaving, because the merchants were bringing Christianity into disrepute and damaging the position of the missionaries in Japan. Sassetti, in a letter from Lisbon dated October 10th, 1578 describes the city, its inhabitants and its merchandise :

> "It remains for me to say that slaves are brought here from all parts.....From elsewhere come the Japanese, an olive-skinned people who understand every art and craft excellently well....the Chinese are men of great intelligence and similarly are skilled in all the arts, but above all learn to cook marvellously...."[2]

Thomas Nelson in his excellent article[3], gives documentary evidence of just how greatly this trade was resented. Unfortunately, the rulers of Spain and Portugal, were too distant and did not have the power to restrain the merchants, and the Church was no more successful, in spite of repeated threats of excommunication.

The Japanese attitude to slavery is interesting. Slavery existed, although the country was not, and had never been, economically slave-dependant. Prisoners of war formed a large part of the slave population and Hideyoshi himself in the course of the Imjin Wars had brought an estimated 65,000+ captives from Korea. Debt slaves existed, as elsewhere in Asia, and some were born into slavery. During the troubled period of the Civil Wars, when law and order were in short supply and labour at a premium, kidnapping either for ransom or to procure workers was not uncommon. Then, there was the issue of girls being sold or indentured by impoverished parents to work as servants or, often, in the sex industry, a pattern that continued into the 20th c and is treated admirably by Amy Stanley in *Selling Women.*

Hideyoshi's objections to the slave trade – besides being a way of attacking the Christians, with whom he was angry for other reasons, and foreigners in general – was partly nationalist: Japanese should not be enslaved by non-Japanese. But there were other aspects, which applied equally to Japanese traders. Slavery was acceptable, in the circumstances mentioned above, but slaving was not and at certain periods carried the death penalty. European experiences with slavery in Japan were mostly formed on Kyushu, where it was much more prevalent than further North: in 1578, Fr. Luís Fróis mentions slaves being sold there in lots of 40. Again, there was a very strong feeling that slavery, when viewed as employment not punishment, should have a definite term, generally ten years. Above all, as Hideyoshi's letter makes clear, people should not be sold to places too far from home and from which they could not return. He himself considered the practice "outrageous" and regularly freed and sent home to their villages people who had been victims of *hitogari* – people harvesting – during the Civil Wars.

Amy Stanley makes some very interesting points about this in the context of girls being sold within Japan for sex work. Great efforts were made, particularly before 1750, to maintain the fiction that the girls were obeying the Confucian moral injunction of filial piety and were sacrificing themselves for their parents. This, of course, had certain advantages: it meant that the girls were not despised and, when their ten years service was up, had a perfectly good chance of a normal marriage. It also meant a feeling that the girls should not be sent so far from home that they could not perform other filial duties, such as visiting the family graves. Conversely, it meant they could be cared for by their families when ill, thus – incidentally – sparing the brothel-keeper medical expenses. Curiously, this was considered particularly important at Nagasaki, a city with a strongly Christian past, which might have been expected to be less charitable than elsewhere towards the Magdalenes in their midst.

[1] Fróis, *Historia de Japam* (vol.4, p.402), and cited Nelson
[2] Sassetti, Letter 56, p.220

Bibliography

Fróis, Luís, *Historia de Japam (1578)*, Lisboa: 1976

Kitahara, Michio, *Portuguese Colonialism and Japanese Slaves*, Tokyo: Kodansha, 2013

Nelson, Thomas "Slavery in Medieval Japan", Monumenta Nipponica 59, No.4 (2004)

Sassetti, Filippo *Lettere da Vari Paesi 1570-1588*, ed.Vanni Bramanti, Longanesi: Milano, 1970, Letter 56, p.220

Stanley, Amy, *Selling women: prostitution, markets and the household in early modern Japan*, University of California Press: Berkeley, 2012

Japanese Contacts with Europe and New Spain, Individual and Diplomatic

The Japanese diplomatic missions to Europe and New Spain excited great interest at the time and have generated a considerable literature. A good deal of this material is readily available, so only a very brief outline will be given here.

Although Japanese are known to have reached Europe and perhaps even New Spain, earlier, as slaves or crew, the first official envoy seems to have been a convert, Bernardo of Kagoshima, who, in 1553 reached Portugal bearing a letter from St Francis Xavier. Bernardo visited Rome and spent four years in Europe, in the course of which he was received into the Jesuit Order; however he died on his way back to Portugal in 1557.

The question of Japanese slavery has already been discussed, but at least one case of Japanese nationals reaching Europe as crew has been documented, and there were almost certainly others. In 1587, the Manila galleon, the *Santa Ana* – a splendid prize – was captured off Baja California by the English privateer and scourge of the Spanish, Thomas Cavendish. He put most of the Spanish ashore, including Sebastián Vizcaíno, who was later to chart California and go as envoy to Japan, but he retained several non-Spaniards. According to the diary kept by his navigator, Francis Pretty, on November 4th, 1587

> "....he took out of this great ship two young lads born in Japan, which could both read and write their own language..."[1]

Their names are given as Christopher and Cosmas (perhaps Cristobal and Gusmão or Cosme), they were Christian and no doubt spoke Portuguese or Spanish.

Three years later, in a complicated anecdote, Christopher and Cosmas are mentioned again, this time by Anthony Knivet[2], as having been with Thomas Cavendish on his ill-fated expedition to Brazil in 1591. This implies that they had spent the intervening three years with him, based in England. Their ultimate fate is unknown. Most probably they died either in Brazil – where Knivet was one of the few survivors – or with Cavendish in the South Atlantic. Just conceivably, they continued on Cavendish's ship with John Davis, his navigator, to discover the Falkland Islands.

Even before the Portuguese reached Japan, or the Spanish established Manila as their capital, there were trade links between the Far East and Central and South America, which may have intersected with Japanese mercantile ventures in the Philippines. Certainly from the mid-16th century, Japanese goods were making their way to the New World and, as has already been said, Ieyasu spent several years trying to persuade successive governors of the Philippines to open up trade opportunities, offering various inducements to the Spanish, such as generous port facilities. These overtures on occasion, oddly enough, put forward by the Englishman Will Adams, were – until the advent of Vivero – ignored. This was largely because of the violent opposition, on the part of both the Portuguese and the Sevillian merchants, to sharing the trade of which they had the monopoly.

It is hardly surprising that the Japanese were anxious to participate actively in trade with both Europe, and Mexico and Peru. In 1603, the Spanish poet, Bernardo de Balbuena praised Mexico in a long poem, which echoed the general perception of the New World[3]. Ieyasu was, initially, very anxious to extend Japan's overseas network and the merchants were well aware of the opportunities offered by countries avid for exotic luxury goods.

Vivero's shipwreck resulted in an informal mission, the subject of the *Relación*. Almost a year later, he embarked for New Spain on August 1st, 1610, on board the *San Buenaventura*, a ship built for the purpose by Will Adams. Accompanying him, were 23 Japanese, headed by Tanaka Shōsuke, who was to take back to Japan information on silver mining technology, so much desired by the Shogun. Vivero was facilitating what was in fact the first Japanese trade mission to the Americas.

There had, of course, been the earlier mission, the Tenshō Embassy of 1582-90, organized by Fr. Alessandro Valignano and sponsored by three Christian daimyos, the most important of whom was Ōtomo Sōrin. It was composed of four young Japanese, headed by Mancio Itō, two servants and their tutor, Fr. Diego de

Mezquita. They visited the Pope and various European rulers, including Philip II of Spain and Francesco de' Medici, Grand Duke of Tuscany. The mission was of great importance, both in bringing Japan to the attention of Europe and in stimulating missionary vocations for the Far East.

The other aim of the mission was to show the young Japanese Christendom, so that they could report on it back home. To this end, a series of dialogues, written as if they were conversations among the young travellers, on aspects of their experiences (the positive side, naturally, being stressed) were published at Macao by the Jesuits to instruct and edify the Japanese community, in line with similar dialogues prepared earlier for the Chinese. On their return to Japan, all four of the young men were ordained and one of them, Julião Nakamura died a martyr in 1633.

The Tenshō Embassy, however, took the Portuguese route via Goa and round Africa to Lisbon and did not touch the New World.

Although the mission that reached Mexico with Vivero on the whole went well, there was, as so often, trouble between the Japanese and the locals. In view of this it is particularly interesting to note the remarkable "Ship's Oath", apparently written by Fujiwara Seiko, Ieyasu's advisor, who prepared much of his diplomatic correspondence, for sailors heading for Annam (Vietnam) c.1610:

> "Foreign lands may differ from our own in manners and speech, but as to the nature bestowed upon men by heaven there cannot be any difference. Do not forget the common identity and exploit differences…In case you meet men of benevolence and education, respect them as you would your own father or teacher. Inquire into the restrictions and taboos of the country, and act in accordance with its customs and religion…Between heaven above and earth beneath all people are brothers and things are the common property of all, everyone being equal in the light of Humanity."[4]

Vivero's unintentional visit to Japan required a return mission, to repay the money lent him by Ieyasu, to repatriate the Japanese contingent and to consolidate the arrangements that he had begun. The man chosen was Sebastián Vizcaíno, known principally today for having carried out the first survey of the California coast. Once in Japan, he asked permission of the *bakufu* (military government) to survey and map the east coast of Japan, so that the Mexico-bound galleons would be less liable to shipwreck. Permission was granted, but Hideyoshi asked Will Adams what he thought of the request. Adams, seeing an opportunity to damage his rivals, answered bluntly that in Europe it would assumed to be a preliminary to invasion.

Matters were not helped by the fact Vizcaíno was both rude and tactless, something which comes through even in his own account, refusing to comply with Japanese ideas of civility and repeatedly stressing that the Spanish were interested in proselytizing not trade. Nevertheless, his unsuccessful negotiations did lead to the largest Japanese embassy to Europe before modern times. The Keichō Embassy was very different from its predecessor and aimed at promoting diplomatic and trade contacts, unlike the Tenshō, which was largely concerned with religion.

After a series of vicissitudes, Vizcaíno finally returned to the New World, as he says himself, as a passenger, without status, on board the *San Juan Battista*[5], a ship again built with advice from Adams. The ship carried 180 passengers, of whom about 140 were Japanese, including 22 samurai, a number of merchants and servants. The mission was headed by Hasekura Rokuemon Tsunenaga, a retainer of the daimyo Date Masamune of Sendai, and accompanied by Fr. Luis Sotelo. Tanaka Shōsuke also visited the west for the second time. The ship arrived at Cape Mendocino in California before going on to Acapulco after three months at sea and some interesting details of the visit are given by the Mexican, Chimalpahin.

Because of the size of the group, not all of the Japanese went on to Europe, but those that did set out via Cuba, reaching Sanlúcar de Barrameda in October, 1614 and continuing on to Seville, where their reception is described in a document in the *Biblioteca Columbina*. It mentions, among other things, that the captain of the Guard was the son of a Japanese martyr, by name Don Thomas. In January, the embassy was in Madrid, where Hasekura – often given as Faxicura – was baptised by the King's chaplain, receiving the names of Felipe Francisco. On the way to Italy, they stopped briefly in Saint-Tropez, where they caused the usual sensation and a number of Japanese customs were recorded by Mme de St Troppez[6].

The embassy in Europe caused great interest and there are a

considerable number of contemporary accounts, notably a work on Japan attributed to Fr. Sotelo and another, published in Rome in 1615 and translated into various languages: *Regno di Voxu*, by Scipione Amati, who accompanied the mission in Italy. There were also several portraits. One, part of a series of portraits of foreign ambassadors painted in 1616 for the Sala degli Ambasciatori of the Palazzo Quirinale in Rome, then a Papal palace, shows Sotelo and Hasekura deep in conversation, surrounded by the other members of the mission. They are in what looks like a distinctly conspiratorial huddle, rather than theological debate, lending credence to the suspicion that their mission was not purely religious.

Nevertheless, while in Rome they were received by the Pope, Paul V, and spent a number of months discussing the dispatch of missionaries to Japan and the opportunities for trade. The Pope referred the latter issue to Philip III of Spain, who refused to sign an agreement because he was – rightly – not sure that the mission came from the ruler of Japan. The Franciscans, on the whole, painted an unrealistically positive picture of Christianity in Japan, coincidentally, at the very moment that Tokugawa Ieyasu's persecutions had intensified.

In June 1617, the mission left Seville for the New World. Some of the Japanese remained behind in nearby Coria del Río, where a number of families with the surname Japón claim descent from them. The remainder of the travelers returned to Mexico, where they found the *San Juan Battista*, which had made a further round trip, bringing Japanese luxury goods for the markets of the New World. Five months later, they set out for the Philippines and in August 1620 reached Nagasaki. Hasekura went on to Sendai, where he met with Date Masamune:

> "Two days after the return of Rokuemon [Hasekura] to Sendai, a three-point edict against the Christian was promulgated: first, that all Christians were ordered to abandon their faith, in accordance with the rule of the Shogun, and for those who did not, they would be exiled if they were nobles, and killed if they were citizens, peasants or servants. Second, that a reward would be given for the denunciation of hidden Christians. Third that propagators of the Christian faith should leave the Sendai fief, or else, abandon their religion"[7]

Persecution of the Christians intensified and Japan moved towards *sakoku* – "chained country" – or total closure. Hasekura died in 1622. In 1623, Tokugawa Hidetada severed trade with Spain and in 1624 – the year in which Fr. Luis Sotelo was martyred – he also put an end to diplomatic relations.

Did Vivero know anything of these developments when he sat down to write his *Relación*, probably in 1627? There is no indication that he did, and yet news of the persecutions and martyrdoms must surely have filtered through to Mexico. Was the *Relación* in fact written earlier? Or, in his busy life, had news of events in the East passed him by?

Especially after the Hasekura visit to Mexico in 1614, Japanese works of art became highly sought after in both Spain and the New World. Screens were particularly popular – Luís de Velasco II owned a set, perhaps a gift from his Japanese visitors, and they were widely imitated with a range of local, as well as traditionally Asian, subjects. Screens were not the only objects that found favour – other small pieces of furniture, such as painted and lacquered writing boxes were extremely popular and attempts were made to imitate them. Very striking too are the numerous images of the Virgin and Saints, and occasionally crucifixes, carved from bone or ivory with markedly Asian features, but these were generally produced by Chinese craftsmen in the Philippines. They were much appreciated by the indigenous populations of Central and South America, who probably found them easier to identify with than those in the purely European tradition.

The question arises, as in the case of certain textile techniques, of how these skills were transmitted. Was it simply imitation? Or did a small number of craftsmen end up in the New World? It is known that Japanese from the mission led by Fr. Sotelo and Hasekura Tsunenaga remained in Spain, but there is some uncertainty as to whether any of those who came to Mexico with Vizcaíno on his return remained permanently in the country. The anthropologist, Zelia Nuttall, writing more than a century ago, points out that in the course of the Japanese diaspora, caused by the religious persecutions, some may have reached the New World from the Philippines. She also postulates that a few artifacts, such as raincoats made of grass or palm leaves – neither European nor pre-Columbian in origin – in use in the Oaxaca region and elsewhere, may have been introduced by Japanese who lingered on in Mexico.

It is, of course, not always easy to identify Christians of Japanese origin, since they generally took purely Hispanic names on baptism, but studies of censuses by Lockhart and others indicate a wide range of nationalities. In a census for 1613 taken at Lima, for example, 38 "chinos" are mentioned, as well as 20 Japanese and 56 from "India de Portugal", which would have implied Goa and Malacca, and perhaps Cambodia. Surprisingly, since immigration to the Spanish colonies was strictly controlled, at least in theory, a contemporary writer describes the wide range of different nationalities thronging the streets of Lima.[8]

[1] Francis Pretty in Richard Hakluyt, *Voyages*, vol.8, London: Everyman, 1907, p.237

[2] Antony Knivet, "The admirable adventures and strange fortunes of Master Antonie Knivet....1591", in Samuel Purchas, *Hakluytus Postumus*, vol.16, New York, 1965, pp.178-9 and 183-4

[3] ¡Oh ciudad rica, puebla sin segundo,
más lleno de tesoros y bellezas
que de peces y arena el mar profundo!
.....
De tesoros y plata tan preñada,
que una flota de España, otra de Cina
de sus sobras cada año va cargada
.....
Al fin, del mundo lo major, la nata
De cuanto se conoce y se practica'
Aquí se bulle, vende y se barata...
    "Grandeza Mexicana", Bernardo de Balbuena, Mexico City: 1603.

[4] *Sources*, vol.1, p.338.

[5] A sketch of the ship appears on the map: "Vista de la ciudad bahía y la ciudad de Acapulco – . D. Un barco que ha llegado de Japón", in *Exploración del mundo*, Nicolás de Cardona, 1632. Bibliotheca National de Madrid.

[6] Marcouin pp114-6

[7] November 1620 letter of Father Angelis, Japan-China archives of the Jesuits in Rome, quoted in Takashi Gonoi's "Hasekura Tsunenaga", Tokyo: 2003, p231

[8] "En Lima y todo el Perú biven y andan gentes de todos los mejores lugares, ciudades y billas de España y gentes de la nación portuguesa, guallegos, asturianos, biscaynas, nabarreses, valencianos, de Murcia, franceses, italianos, alemanes, flamencos, griegas y raguses, corsos, genoveses, mallorquines, canarios, yngleses, moriscos, gente de la Yndia y de la China [generally Philippines] y otras muchas mesclas y misturas..."
Pedro de León Portocarrero "El judío portugués", *Discrición de Lima* (c.1610), cited in *Extremo Oriente* p.225

Bibliography

A Testimony of the 400th Anniversary of Mexico-Japan Relations Special Exhibition: The Dream of Friendship Carried by the Galleons, Tokyo, Tobacco and Salt Museum, 2010

De Bary, William Theodore and Tsunoda, Ryusaku, *Sources of Japanese Tradition: from Earliest Times to 1600, Vol I*, Columbia University Press, 1964

Ellis, Robert Richmond, *They Need Nothing: Hispanic-Asian Encounters of the Colonial Period*, University of Toronto Press, 2012

Falck Reyes, Melba and Palacios, Héctor, *Japanese Merchants in 17th Century Guadalajara*, Revista Iberoamericana, 22.2 (2011), pp.191-237

Fróis, Luís S.J., La première ambassade du Japon en Europe, 1582-1592 *[1597]* ed. and tr. J. A. Abranches Pinto, *Yoshitomo Okamoto and Henri Bernard. Vol. 1*, Tokyo: Sophia University, 1942

Gil, Juan, *Hidalgos y samurais: España y Japón en los siglos XVI y XVII*, Madrid : Alianza Editorial, c1991

Iwasaki, Fernando, *Extremo Oriente y Peru en el siglo XVI*, Mapfre America, Madrid, 1992

Koichi Izumi, José and Gil, Juan, *Historia de la Embajada de Idate Masamune al Papa Paulo V (1613-1615) por el Doctor Escipión Amati*, Madrid: Ediciones Doce Calles, 2011

La Embajada Japonesa de 1614 a la Ciudad de Sevilla, Sevilla: Ayuntamento de Sevilla, 1992

Marcouin, Francis and Keiko Omoto. *Quand le Japon s'ouvrit au monde*. Paris: Découvertes Gallimard, 1990

Massarella, David – detailed bibliography for Japan/Europe contacts available on-line at *www.ames.cam.ac.uk*

Takashi, Gonoi, *Hasekura Tsunenaga*, Tokyo: Yoshikawa Kobunkan, 2003
The documents relating to these missions have been proposed for the *International Memory of the World Register* and are conveniently listed at *www.unesco.org*

The world and Japan: the embassies of Tensho and Keicho Sendai City Museum, 1995.

Valignano, Alessandro, *Japanese Travellers in Sixteenth Century Europe: A dialogue concerning the mission to the Roman Curia (1590)*, ed. Derek Massarella, tr. J.F. Moran, London: Hakluyt Society, 2012

Wikipedia – *Hasekura Tsunenaga* – article with detailed itinerary of the mission, texts in the original languages, bibliography and images

www.ayto-coriadelrio.es – Valencia Japón, Victor, *Hasekura Tsunenaga*

www.japanesembassies.wordpress.com – an excellent and useful checklist of the documents relating to the Tenshō and Keichō embassies with bibliography.

Spain, the Netherlands and England

The tensions between these three countries form the backdrop to Vivero's account and a power struggle that was taking place in Europe, spread to the Far East and the Americas. Although well known, it is still worth giving a very brief outline of the issues.

A key element, of course, was religion. In the early 16th century, the Netherlands formed part of the Holy Roman Empire, ruled from Spain. However, Protestantism in various forms, especially Calvinism, was making inroads in what had been a Catholic country. Philip II of Spain reacted with persecution and in 1568 the Eighty Years War began between the Netherlands and Spain.

England, which had rejected Catholicism under Henry VIII, was Protestant and in 1585, Elizabeth I sent troops to support the Dutch who were seeking independence. The period 1579-81 saw a coalition of northern provinces secede from Spain, while those to the south, where from the late 16th century the Jesuits were very active, remained predominantly Catholic. The Dutch Republic (the Northern States) did not become independent from Spain until 1648, more than a decade after Vivero's death. The Spanish Netherlands, on the other hand, with its capital at Brussels, remained within the Spanish sphere of influence until the 18th century.

Besides the question of religion, this was the period when the Dutch first appeared in Asia and, as Vivero so greatly feared, were to take over almost all of the Portuguese possessions, resulting in grave economic – as well as spiritual – loss. The Dutch, who were concerned with profit not souls, were to build an extremely effective trade empire, dominating exchanges with the Far East for most of the 17th century. This affected Spain as well as Portugal – the two countries having been united since 1580, when the King of Portugal died without an heir. The Iberian Union was not, however, a happy one and only lasted until 1640. These tensions lie in the background of Vivero's account.

It was not only Portuguese and Spanish trade and influence in Asia that were under threat. Much of Vivero's career had been spent trying to defend Spain's possessions in the New World. They were constantly under attack by the English and Dutch pirates, who had become a major problem from the middle of the 16th century, as the wealth of the region became more and more apparent. In his *Advice*, Vivero makes repeated pleas for resources to chase the pirates out of their strongholds in the islands and on the coast of North America, pointing out that unless this were done, cities on the Caribbean would never be safe and the treasure fleet carrying bullion back to Spain would always risk attack. Men like Sir Francis Drake were perceived by the English as national heroes, but by the Spanish as pirates and outlaws, and it is from this perspective that Vivero warned Ieyasu so passionately against allowing the Dutch access to Japan.

Bibliography

Cocks, Richard, *The Diary of Richard Cocks*, [1613-1623], ed. N.Murakami, Tokyo: 1899

González Díaz, Falia, *Mare Clausum. Mare Liberum. La piratería en la América Española*. Archivo General de Indias, Sevilla, 2009

Murakami, Naojiro, *Letters written by English Residents in Japan 1611-1623*, Tokyo: 1900

Saris, John, *The voyage of Captain John Saris to Japan, 1613*, ed. Ernest Satow, London: Hakluyt, 1900

Chimalpahin on the Japanese in Mexico

Surprisingly, a good part of the information on the Japanese who visited Mexico with Vivero and with Vizcaíno comes from the Nahuatl chronicle of Domingo Francisco de San Antón Muñón Chimalpahin Quauhtlehuanitzin (1579-1660), generally known as Chimalpahin. The references given below are all from the excellent edition and translation: *Annals of His Time* published at Stanford.

The first reference to Vivero and the Japanese dates from February 1610 when news came that he had "perished on the ocean." Chimalpahin also relates that:

> "...don fray Pedro de Agurto, bishop of Japan, who was an Augustinian friar, passed away there. He was born here in Mexico, a child of people here. He is thought to have been the only *criollo* made a bishop yet; he started it that children of people here are ascending and ruling."

He goes on to mention that Vivero should have been on his way from the Philippines, "but he perished on the ocean as became known". p.163

Chimalpahin generally uses the term *criollo* to mean a Spaniard born in the New World – in which case it would in fact also have applied to Vivero.

His next reference to Vivero is dated Monday, 15th November 1610 "...when don Rodrigo de Vivero entered Mexico here..." Chimalpahin gives quite an accurate summary of Vivero's experiences, again adding that it had been rumoured that Vivero had died at sea. He ends by saying:

> "When he entered here in Mexico, it was just by himself; he left behind on the road the Japanese who were coming here and leaving Japan to come at their leisure after they had landed at the port of Acapulco; don Rodrigo hurried ahead of them." pp.168-9

A month later, he provides a more detailed description:

> "Today, Thursday in the afternoon, the 16th of the month of December of the year 1610, at 6 o'clock, perhaps as many as

nineteen people from Japan, in China [the term was often used for the Philippines] arrived and entered here in the city of Mexico. A noble, their lord, the ambassador, from the court of the great ruler the emperor of Japan, who brought them, came to make peace with the Christians so that they would never make war but always be at peace and esteem each other, so that Spanish merchants will be able to enter Japan and none of the people there will be able to impede them, for thus the lord Viceroy don Luìs de Velasco, Marqués os Salinas, whom they came to see, informed them. Don Rodrigo de Vivero brought them here; they had all landed together; he had gone to be governor in the city of Manila in China...."

Vivero's adventures are related again in more detail, including the loan made to him in Japan to enable him to return home.

"...And also because of that don Roderigo came bringing people of Japan to come and get the so and so many thousand pesos that he borrowed. And some of the said people of Japan who came here were already Christians and some still idolaters who were not yet baptized. And they came gotten up as they are gotten up there; they wear something like an ornamented jacket, doublet or long blouse, which they tie at their middle, their waist; there they place a catana [Asian cutlass] of metal, which counts as their sword, and they wear something like a mantilla. And their footwear is soft, softened leather called chamois, counting just like foot-gloves that they put on their feet. They seem bold, not gentle and meek people, going about like eagles. And their foreheads are very bare because they closely shave their foreheads, making the shaving of their foreheads reach to the middle of their heads..."p.172

Chimalpahin was clearly fascinated by the way the Japanese wore their hair and describes it at length and also by the homogeneity of their appearance – in Colonial Mexico, every racial mixture was carefully classified and Chimalpahin uses a number of these terms: *castizo, morisco, mulatto*, etc., so a nation that all had the same colouring, like the *indios*, would have been striking.

"And they do not have beards and they have faces like women, and they are whitish and light, with whitish or yellowish faces. All the people of Japan are like that, that is how their corporal aspect is, and they are not very tall, as everyone saw them. When they entered Mexico here, the nobleman from there who came appointed as the leader of the Japan people were greatly honored. The carriage of the viceroy, his very own property, went to Chapoltepec to meet him as he as he was passing by on the road. He sent to him, sitting in the coach together, a Discalced friar whom they brought from Japan, who came to interpret for them, and a judge of the Audiencia who went to Chapoltepec to meet him, when the Japanese came by on the way here. And when they came from Chapoltepec, inside the said carriage rode all three of them, the nobleman from Japan, the Discalced friar and the judge. When they entered the city of Mexico, they came to establish themselves next to the Augustinian church, and not until the next day did they see the lord viceroy; and while they stayed here in Mexico, it was the viceroy who fed them." pp.172-3.

On the 7th of March, 1611,

"....Sebastián Vizcaíno, citizen of Mexico, set out and left Mexico here, appointed general of the China boats going to China [the Philippines]. At that time he then took the Japanese; he placed next to himself the Japanese nobleman whose name was now don Alonso and who now went dressed as a Spaniard, to return to his home; here he threw away his outfit that he wore coming here. He was the only one to change [his clothing] here in Mexico. They had been here in Mexico just two months when seventeen of them returned home; three stayed here in Mexico." pp.174-5

On the 13th March, 1613 news came of the Manila galleon reaching Acapulco and "…on it a Spanish señor Sebastián Vizcaíno , who left Mexico here two years ago…" He was returning from Japan and according to Chimalpahin with a hundred Japanese, an ambassador, "and a Discalced Franciscan friar came along to interpret for them." p236-7.

"Today, Tuesday the 4th of the month of March of the year 1614, was when again there arrived here and entered inside the city of Mexico those Japanese nobles; they came in on horseback at 12 o'clock noon. Their vassals came ahead of them, just coming on foot, holding high something like little long narrow black poles, maybe their lances; perhaps that signifies royal leadership there in Japan. They came attired just the same way they go about and are attired back a home; they wear something like a tunic, tied at the back, and they tie their hair at the backs of their necks. So far only twenty of them have reached Mexico here; they left behind, still coming along the way, the lordly emissary, the ambassador, the messenger sent here by the great ruler the emperor of Japan, who is still coming at his leisure, bringing a hundred of his Japanese vassals. One of our fathers, a Discalced Franciscan friar, comes interpreting for them. This is the second time that the Japanese have landed one of their ships on the shore at Acapulco; they are transporting here everything of iron, and writing desks, and some cloth that they are to sell here. On the said Japanese ship came also señor Sebastián Vizcaíno, a Spaniard, citizen of Mexico, who had gone to Japan to look around, [since] he had taken back the other group of Japanese who had come from there three years ago now, whom don Rodrigo de Vivero who was to be governor in the city of Manila in China, had brought here. The said señor Sebastián Vizcaíno is also still coming slowly, coming hurt; the Japanese injured him when they beat and stabbed him at Acapulco, as became known here in Mexico..." p.276

Chimalpahin goes on to say that Vizcaíno had been entrusted with gifts from the emperor to the king of Spain, the Pope and the viceroy and that he, rather than the ambassador, had been given great responsibilities – perhaps the cause of the quarrel.

On the 24th, he tells us that the ambassador:

"...was settled in a house next to the church of San Francisco. It became known here in Mexico and was said the reason their ruler the emperor in Japan sent this said lordly emissary and ambassador here is to go to Rome to see the holy Father, Paul V, and to give him their obedience concerning the holy church, so that all the Japanese want to become Christians; they are to be baptized, so that they will also be children of our mother the holy Roman Church in matters of the holy sacraments and will always obey it in matters of divinity and faith. And when the great universal spiritual shepherd the holy Father, our universal governor and caretaker, has accepted them, they too will be his sheep. He will see and become acquainted with those who did not belong to him and who he did not know, who had just wandered lost somewhere in the thickets, the plains, the mountains, and lived bestially, who now are converted and go towards him to become acquainted with the really true universal shepherd and place themselves in his hands, so that he will guard, govern, and take care of them too with and in the true unified belief, the holy Catholic faith, so that the devil will never seize them again and make them his through idolatry and worship of devils, in which they are now still, although there are already many Christians there. And this said ambassador who reached Mexico here is just quickly passing through here now, he will stay here only a few days to see the lord viceroy quickly. And also he will pass quickly by our great ruler the king don Felipe III to see him and offer him peace, because their ruler who serves as emperor in Japan to show friendship has established eternal peace toward the said king who is in Spain, so that they will never make war on each other but will always love each other, so that the Japanese can come here to Mexico to act as merchants and sell things. And once this ambassador has seen the king in passing, he is to go on beyond that to Rome….." pp.276-7.

Chimalpahin's rose-coloured view of Christian prospects in Japan accords perfectly with Vivero's account, but clearly he had not heard about the increasingly serious persecutions, which were to result in the Decree of Expulsion in this same year.

On the 25th of April, on the Feast of St Mark, the Archbishop

"…gave holy confirmation to and it was received by the above mentioned Japanese who became new Christians here; 63 people received confirmation. One of their nobles received confirmation, and he was aided by licenciado Vallecillo, the royal prosecutor for civil matters, who became the spiritual father, the sponsor." pp.278-9

In the following month, May 29th,

"…the said lordly emissary, the ambassador from Japan, set out and left for Spain. In going he divided his vassals; he took a certain number of Japanese, and he left an equal number here as merchants to trade and sell things. As the said ambassador left Mexico here to go to Spain he took along a Spaniard, whose name cannot be established, a brother of Doctor Martínez, who by order of the viceroy here went appointed as his secretary because he knows the language of the Japanese, for he went to live among them when he was a soldier." pp.282-3

On the 14th of October, Chimalpahin writes that

"…some Japanese set out from Mexico here going home to Japan; they lived here in Mexico for four years. Some still remained here; they earn a living trading and selling here the goods they brought with them from Japan." pp. 290-1

And on the 7th of February 1615:

"…ten Japanese set out from Mexico here to go to home to Japan; they came here to Mexico to act as merchants." pp.294-5.

The *Annals* come to end in October, 1615 with, appropriately, an account of the measures taken to defend Acapulco against the English about whom Vivero had so frequently expressed warnings:

"....news came, brought by courier from Acapulco, how five ships [of pirates?] are going about on the ocean there; they call them Englishmen, people from England, wicked people, wrong believers called heretics. It was said they came there to wait for the coming of the ship from China [the Philippines], and there they will rob it of all the goods it is bringing..." pp.304-5

Bibliography

Annals of His Time, Domingo Francisco de San Antón Muñón Chimalpahin Quauhtlehuanitzin, ed. and tr. James Lockhart, Susan Schroeder and Doris Namala, Stanford University Press, 2006

Will Adams

William Adams (1564-1620) is mentioned several times by Vivero. Their acquaintance dated from negotiations over trade with Japan in 1608, while Vivero was governor of the Philippines, and continued after his shipwreck. It was in fact in a ship built by Adams that Vivero finally returned to Mexico. Judging by his remarks, Vivero liked and respected Adams, but seems not to have realised that Adams, a Protestant, was even more dangerous than the hated Dutch when it came to influencing the Shogun against the Catholic presence in Japan.

Adams is the first known Englishman to have reached Japan and, besides his surviving letters, which have been published, he has inspired several novels and biographies. It is therefore only necessary to say a few words about him. Trained in shipbuilding and navigation at Limehouse, Adams saw naval service in various capacities, including under Sir Francis Drake against the Spanish Armada in 1588, and later became a pilot for the Barbary Company. In 1598, he was employed by a Dutch company and set sail for the Far East. In 1600, his ship, the *Liefde*, reached Kyushu with only 20 survivors of the original crew. Tokugawa Ieyasu, not yet Shogun, imprisoned them and, according to Jesuit sources, the ship's cannons were used by him at the decisive battle of Sekigahara.

In spite of the Jesuits' efforts to discourage contact, accusing the Dutch, including Adams, of being basically pirates, Ieyasu took a liking to Adams, in large part because of his knowledge of shipbuilding, navigation and mathematics, and gradually he displaced Fr. Rodrigues as the Shogun's official interpreter. In 1603, Ieyasu ordered Adams to build him a European-type ship and another in 1610, the *San Buenaventura*, in which Vivero returned to Mexico with Tanaka Shosuke and twenty-two Japanese, essentially a trade mission.

Ieyasu would never allow Adams to return home, but made him a samurai with the name Miura Anjin and a *hatamoto* – bannerman

– a position of some prestige, with a fief in Hemi. Adams was given a Red Seal License to trade in South East Asia in 1614 and 1615. He was involved in the short-lived English Factory in Japan, although his relationship with his difficult and trouble-prone compatriots was not an easy one, in part because they felt he was "too Japanese", as both Richard Cocks and John Saris complained. Adams, on the other hand, seems to have remained remarkably patient and forbearing. Although he remarried in Japan, Adams never forgot his English family, sending money to them whenever he could and sharing his possessions equally between them and his Japanese family in his will.

Bibliography

Adams, William, *The original letters of the English pilot, William Adams : written from Japan between A.D. 1611 and 1617,* Yokohama : Japan Gazette Office, 1896.

Cocks, Richard, *The Diary of Richard Cocks,* [1613-1623], ed. N.Murakami, Tokyo: 1899

Corr, William, *Adams the pilot: the life and times of Captain William Adams, 1564-1620,* Folkestone : Japan Library, 1995

Saris, John, *The voyage of Captain John Saris to Japan, 1613,* ed. Ernest Satow, London: Hakluyt, 1900

Luis Sotelo

Blessed Luis Sotelo (1574-1624) was a Franciscan friar, born in Seville and educated at Salamanca, who was sent out to the Philippines in 1600. There he ministered to the Japanese community at Dilao on the outskirts of Manila, learning the language and acting as an intermediary during the Japanese attempted rebellion in 1606-7.

In 1608, the Pope authorized the Franciscans and Dominicans to go to Japan, previously the exclusive preserve of the Jesuits. As soon he could, Sotelo set sail. He found favour with the powerful daimyo Date Masamune of Sendai, whose sympathy for the Christians probably had as much to do with his political and mercantile ambitions as with theology. Sotelo should have led the 1610 mission to Europe, but was prevented by ill-health and his place taken by another Franciscan, Fray Alonso Muñoz.

Always controversial, Sotelo ignored the carefully negotiated dispositions of the Jesuits and, flouting the orders of the Shogun, proceeded to build a new church in Tokyo in 1613. As a result, seven Japanese Christians among his followers were arrested and executed. Sotelo was saved through the intervention of Date Masamune.

Partly to get him out of the country, given his propensity for trouble, Sotelo was chosen as interpreter for Date Masamune's embassy to Europe, headed by Hasekura Tsunenaga – their portraits are to be seen in the famous painting in the Palazzo Quirinale in Rome – which set out in the autumn of 1613. Travelling via Acapulco and Veracruz, they visited various cities in Spain, notably Seville and Madrid, before going on to Rome. Sotelo's mission was complicated by a number of factors, including rivalries among the religious Orders, and reluctance of the Spanish authorities to liberalise trade with Japan, as Tokugawa Ieyasu wished and for which Vivero had tried to negotiate.

It was not until 1618 that Sotelo and Hasekura Tsunenaga returned to the east, again via Veracruz and Acapulco. Most of the

Japanese on the mission who had converted to Christianity stayed on in Spain, settling at Coria del Rio outside Seville, where a number of families bearing the surname Japón claim descent from them. Sotelo reached the Philippines in 1620. Date Masamune was anxious for him to return and he succeeded in reaching Japan in 1622, in spite of the absolute prohibition on members of the Religious Orders entering the country. In 1624, he was burned at the stake in punishment and in 1867 was beatified by Pope Pius IX, so that he is known as Blessed Luis Sotelo.

Bibliography

Apostolado y martirio del Beato Luis Sotelo en el Japón, Madrid, 1924

Pagès, Léon, *Histoire de la Religion Chrétienne au Japon depuis 1598 jusqu'a 1651....* Paris, 1869 (pp.137-161 – Letters of Luìs Sotelo)

An Account of the Kingdom of Japan and Information Concerning It

In the year 1608[1], on the 30th of September, the day of the glorious St Jerome, the *San Francisco*, on which I was sailing from the Philippines, where I had served His Majesty in the government of those islands, was lost.

A lengthy account could be given of all the numerous storms and dangers of wreckage that we encountered in the sixty-five days of our voyage before that unlucky hour and I do not know whether such misadventures were ever endured in the northern or the southern seas. But the end of these troubles proved the beginning of others, for the ship went to pieces on the reefs at the furthest point of Japan[2], which lies at 35½º latitude. All the marine charts that show the point to which we had sailed make the very grievous error of locating this headland of Japan at 33½°. To sum up, for this reason – or for the true and original cause, which was to fulfil the will of God – the galleon was lost with merchandise to the value of two million.

From ten o'clock at night when the ship struck land until half an hour after dawn on the following day, all of us who had escaped the wreck were clinging to the rigging and ropes, because the ship was going to pieces. The bravest of us awaited a certain end, that same end which had come for the fifty people who were drowned, born away by the waves and fury of the sea. Among those who were saved through the great mercy of God, some clung to pieces of timber, others to planks and the last were those who managed to remain on part of the poop which was the strongest section and the one which remained most intact until it reached the land. That is where I was and I considered myself rich to be among those who escaped with their shirt.

No one knew whether it was a desert island or indeed where we might be, for the pilots said that judging by the latitude it could not be Japan, so I ordered two sailors to climb up and try to see something of the countryside. They soon returned asking me for a reward [i.e. for bearing good news]: that there were fields sown with rice. This guaranteed us food, but not our lives, for we had no arms or any human means of defence, if to our misfortune the people of the island had not been what in fact they were. Within a quarter of an hour, some Japanese appeared which gave rise to general joy and pleasure, to me in particular.

When I was Governor of the Philippines, it so happened that the *Real Audiencia*, which was in power before my arrival, held two hundred Japanese[3] prisoners. There was no doubt justification for this when they were taken, but since in the fullness of time they produced acceptable reasons for their conduct, I decided not only to free them from prison, but also to give them passage and safe conduct to their own country, for which the emperor[4] had shown himself to be most grateful. I was sure this would not be forgotten and I strongly hoped that he would prove grateful, as was indeed the case.

Five or six Japanese then arrived, the very ones I had pointed out to my companions, showing in both words and gestures that they were most grieved to see us in such a state. By the agency of a Japanese Christian who had been wrecked with me, I asked them where we were and they answered in a few words: in Japan and at a village called Yubanda[5], which was a league and a half from there[6]. We set out thence, cold and shivering, for we were already at the beginning of winter, which in those islands is harsh. And with what clothing we had, we reached the village. It is one of the least of all the hamlets of that island and I think it is the most isolated and poor of the whole kingdom, for it has no more than three hundred inhabitants, vassals of the lord and *tono*[7] of Hondaque[8]. Although he is not one of the richest in terms of revenues, he has many vassals and villages under his sway, and an impregnable fortress, which I will describe later.

Having reached this wretched place, the interpreter of their nation who was with me told them that I was the Governor of Luzon, as they call the Philippines, and related our unlucky journey. They showed great sympathy and the women wept, for they are exceedingly tender-hearted and they had the idea of asking their husbands to lend us some of the clothes which they call kimono[9], lined with cotton. They agreed most generously and even gave me some. They were also liberal in giving us the food that they themselves eat – that is to say rice and some vegetables such as radishes and eggplant and on rare occasions fish, for fishing is very difficult along that coast.

Then they informed the lord and *tono* of the village, who lived six leagues away and he ordered that I should be well treated, but that I should not be allowed to go out, nor any of those who were with me. As I understood it from my host where I was lodging, before this communication they had gathered together and decided to cut our throats, but God, Who had saved us from greater tempests, calmed this one too.

Three or four days later, the Lord and *tono* of this land came to visit me with the greatest ceremony. He was preceded by three hundred men bearing different insignia, like those of the *Daire*[10] and King of Japan, each gentleman in accordance with his rank and condition. Most of these men who accompanied him came with lances and arquebuses and with weapons called *naginata*[11], which look something the halberds that we use here, but made of steel and stronger and better.

Before entering the place, he sent one of his household, who entered with more than thirty people, to tell me that he was coming to pay me a visit. On my replying that I would see him with great pleasure, he went out to give my answer to his master. Shortly after came another, with greater ceremony than the first and with a greater train of followers. He came in to see me and the message he brought was that his master the *tono* kissed my hands. He was already in the vicinity and the closer he approached, the greater his pleasure at being about to see me. It seemed to me that in order to comply with the customs of the place, I would have to send someone out to greet him.

My man met up with him near where I was staying. The *tono* received him in the most friendly and courteous manner and answered him as might the finest courtier from the court at Madrid. He dismounted from the very excellent horse that he was riding and called another of his servants, who entered with yet more pomp than any of the others to tell me that his lord was coming. I went out to receive him and seeing me, he stopped and saluted me with his head and a gesture of his hand for this is their customary form of greeting like our bow. There was then a long moment as each tried to rival the other in courtesy, to decide who was to take the best place, which among the Spaniards is the right hand, but in Japan, on the contrary, is the left. They say that this is because it is the side of the sword and that only a very great friend is so trusted[12]. In the end he forced me to take the best place and on going through doors he said to me that they always consider it a greater honour to go behind, because it was said that if a man were not a very great friend, no one would trust him enough to turn their face away.

When we came to sit down, he did the same, placing me in the best seat and began to condole with me on my losses with such discretion and such tactful remarks that I had not a little trouble in answering him. He brought me as a gift four robes which, as I said before, are called kimono, made of damask and other materials, worked in gold and silk, and lined with cotton – very remarkable and in their style of dress most elegant. He also gave me a sword called a *katana*[13], a cow and some chickens and some of the fruit of the region, which is excellent. Also some rice wine and I do not believe there is any to compare with it, except that made of grapes.

This gift was no small thing and of great help to me at that time. He also did something else very generous and worthy of mention: he ordered that until the emperor should give orders as to what was to become of me and the three hundred men who were there, he would feed us all at his own expense, which indeed was done for the thirty-seven days stay in his village. He gave me permission to send two people to the prince and the emperor with news of what had happened to me. I did this, sending the second lieutenant Anton Pequeño and Captain Sevicos with letters.

Although the court of the prince[14] was forty leagues away in the city of Yendo [Edo, modern Tokyo][15] and from there to Surunga[16], where the emperor[17] his father resided, was another forty, and although such a novel affair could not fail to cause difficulties, the governors of Japan and the ministers of their kings are so swift in handling affairs that within twenty days my messengers returned. With them came a man from the household of the prince within whose jurisdiction the matter fell, although even he did not dare to make any arrangements without informing his father. The *chapas*[18] that they sent me are like royal ordinances showing that the emperor had been informed. And it was on his orders that the member of the royal household whom I mentioned before came to tell me on behalf of them both that they greatly regretted my loss.

78

They would send dispatches in order that the goods on the beach, which had been rescued from the ship, would be made over to me, and so that I could proceed to the court of the prince and the emperor. It was also arranged that the authorities and governors along the way would offer me hospitality, give me aid and generally make me welcome. According to the laws of the kingdom, the goods from the wrecked ship, that they had ordered to be given to me, belonged to the prince, for one law stated that whatever was on board any ship, whether foreign or native, that was lost off Japan and washed up on her shores, was the property of the king[19]. But, since it was his own possession, he did me the great kindness of giving it to me and had the keys of the warehouses where it was stored made over to me, so that I could subsequently take possession of it and do with it whatever I wished.

A difference arose among us as to whether the emperor had the right to give me these things and whether I in good conscience could accept them. Although it was the time when I was in worst straits of all my life and there was no lack of arguments on my side, having considered every aspect, I received the keys and handed them over to the captain and master of the ship, so that he could send back the goods and merchandise to Manila, or wherever they came from, and return them to their rightful owners.

At this point, I set off for the city of Yendo and on the first stage reached a place with ten or twelve thousand inhabitants called Ondaque[20]. Having stopped at an inn, the *tono* sent to me with the request that I should stay at his house and that he would soon come to fetch me. This forced me to go to him at his place, which was at the highest point of the town.

Entering by the first gate, there was a moat more than fifty *estados*[21] deep with a drawbridge. When it was raised, it seemed impossible, or at least extremely difficult, to reach the gate of the fortress. Given that this site by nature, or at least with very little artifice, is almost impregnable, I was all the more surprised that as I advanced further into the castle I saw gates, entirely made of iron and very large. In front of the moat, there was something like an embanked wall of earth more than six *baras*[22] high and the same in width. At this gate stood a hundred or so arquebusiers, their weapons in their hands and as ready to fire as if the enemy were upon them.

About a hundred paces further on, there was another strong door with another smaller masonry wall built of larger worked stones and between the first gate and the second, there were houses, orchards and gardens sown with rice, so that even if the fortress were besieged it could support itself for several months. At this second gate, there must have been thirty men with lances. Their captain, showing the greatest courtesy, accompanied me on up, some forty or fifty paces, to the point where the palace and the house of the *tono* began.

He was waiting for me there at the first gate, with fifteen or twenty of his household, and having spoken to me and told me that I was very welcome to his house, he went ahead of me through five or six rooms and chambers, leaving some of his people to guide me. These living quarters were entirely built of wood, for in Japan stone is not normally used for the places where great lords live and sleep, for fear of the terrible earthquakes. However, they work it with greatest skill and they have so many different hues of gold, silver and colours, not only on the ceiling, but everywhere from the floor up, that there is always something to entertain the eye. I reached the room where the *tono* was and after having sat and talked for a while, he showed me his armoury, which seemed more fitting for a king than for a private gentleman.

Then it was time to eat and he got up and brought me the first dish, a custom much in use in Japan, as showing the affection they bear their guests. There was meat, fish and fruit and an abundance of other delicacies. Having risen from table and rested for a while, I took my leave to go and sleep two leagues distant. He gave me a horse, so that the journey would be easier for me. From that day, until I saw him again at the court of the prince more than six months later, he always wrote to me and we maintained the friendship that had begun there.

In the thirty leagues or so leading up to the city of Yendo, which, as I have said, is the court of the prince, there, is nothing noteworthy to describe. The places along the way[23] are larger and the multitude of people excited our admiration, but since we later saw far more than there, we can leave the matter aside. Everywhere they gave me lodging, looked after me and treated me with all the love that would be lavished on the person in the kingdom whom their King most esteemed.

The day that I was to reach the court and the famous city of Yendo, numerous horsemen rode out to invite me to be their guest, but I could not choose, because on the orders of the prince I already had a lodging place. I arrived there at five in the evening, accompanied by a crowd of those who had come out to receive me, as well as people of the city, attracted by the novelty of foreigners wearing clothes the like of which they had never seen before. As a result, in order to advance, it was necessary to hold them back and force one's way along the streets, although they are very wide. Word of the new arrivals spread through the city, so that in the eight days that I was in the city on that first occasion, I was not left in peace for a single moment. Although there was no way to escape the visits of people of note, in order to get the common people to let me eat or rest a little, I had to have recourse to the secretary of the prince, who put a guard on the door and issued a proclamation, saying that no one was to enter without my permission.

Although the city of Yendo does not have as many people as certain others in Japan, it has some remarkable qualities for which it is famous, which I will describe insofar as I remember them.[24] This city has a hundred and fifty thousand inhabitants; as well as the sea beating against the foot of the houses, a great river runs through the middle of the city and brings with it fair-sized boats, although ships cannot enter because there is not enough depth[25].

Along this river, which is tidal and flows along many streets, come most of the provisions, so conveniently and cheaply that a man can eat reasonably for half a real[26] a day. Although the Japanese do not eat bread, except as an exotic luxury for dessert[27], it is not an exaggeration to say that what they make in that town is the best in the world and, because little is bought, it is almost given away.

There is a great deal to see in the streets and general location of the town and its administration gives much food for thought, for it would bear comparison with that of the Romans. Few of the streets are better than the others, rather there is great equality and they are wide, long and straight, much more so than those of our own Spain. The houses are of wood and some have an upper storey, although not all. Granted that ours appear better from the outside, the perfection of theirs within gives them an immense advantage. And the cleanliness of the streets is such that one would say that no one ever walks there.

They all have gates[28]and the streets are completely distinct, according to the different crafts and craftsmen. In one street there are carpenters, without any other trade or craftsmen being allowed to mix with them, in another shoemakers, blacksmiths, merchants and, to sum up, in all the streets and all the quarters there is to be found every possible craft and trade that can be imagined, including many that in Europe do not exist or that we are not accustomed to see. The same is true of the merchants, for those who deal in silver have their quarter and those in gold likewise, and those in silk and other goods likewise, without one trade ever being seen in the street of another.

There is a special street and place for game such as partridges and geese, ducks[29], cranes, hens and all kinds of feathered creatures in great abundance. In another street, are other kinds of game, such as rabbits, hares, wild boar and venison in incredible quantity. In another quarter, there is what they call the fish market and they took me there out of interest, so that I could see it. There they sell every kind of sea and river fish that anyone could want: dry, salt and fresh and in very large tubs full of water great quantities of live fish, so that each can buy what he wants, according to his taste. As there are so many of them, the sellers accost one in the street and lower their prices, depending on the time and the need in which they find themselves.

There are streets where they sell and rent out horses and they are so numerous that when a traveller arrives – it is the custom to change horses every two leagues – many come out to offer them and show off the paces of their horses, so one hardly knows how to choose.

The street and quarter of bad women is always to be found on the outskirts of the place.[30]

Nobles and gentlemen live in their own streets and quarters apart from the rest of the population and therefore they do not mix with the common people, or those who are not of their quality. They [the upper classes] are easily recognized by the gilded and painted weapons over the doors of their houses and they spend so much on this, that there are doorways that have cost more than twenty thousand ducats.[31]

As regards the political government of the city, there is a governor who is superior to all the other magistrates – However, each street has two gates, one at the entrance and one at the exit, and the most suitable and well-considered man of all those in the street is chosen as headman and justice of the peace for that street. He is responsible for all the civil and criminal disputes, both to inflict punishment and, in serious or difficult cases, refer them to the governor. The law, which comes above all else with them, is that they may admit neither prayers nor intercession from their superiors or their inferiors, which might prevent them from administering justice. These streets are shut each night at dusk and there are always soldiers at their post day and night, so that if a crime is committed, the news is passed on by word of mouth, by shouting, and in the briefest time the gates are shut and the criminal trapped within and punished.

Although I am talking about the city of Yendo and the court of the prince[32], the same is true and established in all the other cities of the kingdom, both as regards political government and everything else. Since most of these cities are on the sea, they also have the great advantage of abundant fish, for they do not eat meat, except game killed in the hunt, for otherwise it is against their laws.[33] In this city of Yendo, the prince has allowed the monastery of St Francis, of the Discalced Friars, to be publicly recognized. It is the only one in the kingdom to have such permission, for there are no other openly visible churches – all the others appear to be ordinary homes.[34]

Two days after I had arrived and the prince having twice sent his General of the Sea[35] to visit me, he informed me by way of his secretary, Consecundono[36], that I could go and kiss his hands, which I did at four o'clock in the afternoon. It would be really impossible for me to describe the splendour of this royal palace[37] and its surrounding buildings, both in material terms and because of the numerous horsemen and soldiers who were gathered at the palace that day. Without any doubt, between the first gate and the apartments of the prince, there were more than twenty thousand people, not gathered there by chance, but members of the household, wearing the family crest and serving in the palace in different capacities.

The first and principal wall is made of very large square stones cut and built into a wall without lime or any kind of mortar. It is extremely thick and has embrasures through which to fire the artillery, of which they have some pieces, although few[38]. Below this wall there is a moat, which the river beats upon and a drawbridge, the best designed that I have ever seen. The gates are strong and having opened them for me, they revealed two lines of arquebusiers and musketeers. It seemed to me that there were more than a thousand men and if I am not mistaken, that is what their captain said, who accompanied me to the second gate; the distance between the two was three hundred paces. There I saw another kind of wall forming a rampart and a company of men armed with pikes and lances numbering about four hundred.

They took me to the third gate, which has another stone wall four *baras*[39] high and along this there are at intervals outworks like ravelins for the arquebuses and muskets. There was another company, some three hundred in number, bearing *naginata*, which are like halberds. These men and the others have their houses in the spaces between these three walls with very pretty gardens; their windows look out on to the town.

From the third gate begins the entrance into the royal palace and on one side there are stables with more than two hundred horses. They are very well treated and fat, and if there had been someone to train them as in Spain, they would have lacked for nothing. They were attached by two lengths of chain, each horse with its rump turned to the wall and their heads turned to face the entrance to the stables, so that there would be no danger of being kicked.

On the other side, is the prince's armoury rich in gilded corselets of the kind they use, pikes, lances, arquebuses, *katanas* and enough weapons to arm a hundred thousand men.[40] Further on, there is the first hall of the palace and one cannot see the floor, the walls or the ceiling. On the floor they have what are called *tatami*[41], which are like rush mats, but much prettier, with the edges decorated with cloth of gold and figured satin and velvet with many golden flowers. They are square like a desk and fit together, again with a high degree of workmanship. The walls, which are all made of wood have panels decorated to blend with them, displaying various hunting scenes in gold, silver and colours. The ceiling is the same, so that one does not see the white of the wood anywhere. And although it seemed to us foreigners that nothing more could be wished for than what was seen in this first room, yet the second room was better and the third even more remarkable. Always, the further on into the palace one went, the more curiosities were to be seen and the greater the richness. From each of these apartments, numerous gentlemen and knights came out to greet me and according to what I understood they only had permission to go a certain distance and not pass beyond the doors or places assigned to them, for where one group left me, another received me.

The prince was waiting for me in a great chamber, in the middle of which there were three steps. Six or eight paces further on, he was sitting on the floor on one of the mats that I mentioned before on a square cloth, like a carpet of crimson velvet trimmed with gold. He was dressed in green and yellow, wearing two of the garments they call *kimono* and girded over them were his sword and dagger, which are known as *katana*. On his head, he had nothing but some coloured ribbons plaited into his hair. He is a man thirty-five years old[42], dark skinned but with a fine face and of a fair height.

The secretaries ordered the people who had come with me to remain where they were and thus I entered alone with the pair of them. They took me to where I was to sit, which was on the floor, like the prince and to his left. He then told me to cover my head and smiling said, through the interpreters, that he was happy to see me and get to know me, but sorry that my losses should be making me melancholy. Great men, he added, should not be saddened by the twisted turns of events that were no fault of theirs, and I should feel heartened at finding myself in his kingdom, where he would favour me with whatever I should ask.

I thanked him for this and answered him as best I could. He kept me for more than half an hour, asking me a number of questions about navigation and about my ship and at the end I asked permission to leave on the following day for the court of his father, the emperor. He told me that I could not go next day, but he would allow me to go four days later, because he wanted to notify him first and also give orders that I should be lodged and received along the way as my position merited. At this, he said farewell and dismissed me, and I went back to my lodgings for it was already late. Four days later, I set out for the court at Surunga, forty leagues from Yendo.

I would have no difficulty in describing the cities which I saw along the way, their size and points of interest, but in order not to waste time, I will only say that a place that has twenty thousand heads of households[43] is called a village and that all along the roads from one court to the other, and even from Surunga to the city of Miyako[44], a matter of hundred leagues, there is not so much as a quarter of a league uninhabited. Every time the traveller raises his head, he sees large numbers of people coming and going in the normal way just as in our country. On either side of the road there is a line of pine trees, so shady and pleasant that the sun rarely troubles travellers and there is no need to ask distances for they are measured out. At the end of each league, there is a little circle with two trees[45] and if the end of the league falls in the middle of a street, they pull down the houses and put up the sign, without lengthening or shortening the measurement, for that they will do as a favour to no human alive.

At last, I reached Surunga having travelled for five days and, thanks to the prince was so well received and lodged wherever I went, that if it were not for the fear of ending my days among the pagans and if they were subjects of my king, I would renounce my country for theirs. I will speak briefly about what happened to me at Surunga. The city of Surunga has a hundred and twenty thousand households and, although it does not have such fine streets and houses as Yendo, the climate is considered better and for that reason Taikosama[46] chose it as his place of residence. One of his household came out to receive me at the gates of the town and to show me the inn where I was to lodge. I reached it in the same storm that had engulfed me in other places, with the uproar of the people excited by the arrival of strangers. Indeed, there were so many following us that it was very difficult to make our way along the streets.

The day after my arrival, the emperor sent one of his secretaries to visit me with twelve robes and garments of the kind he wore himself, with many flowers of gold and different coloured silks. The secretary told me that the emperor was very happy to have me at his court. He wanted to know how I was and urged me to rest and put on the robes and garments, because he thought that having emerged from the sea naked, the best gift he could send me would be something to wear. He remained for a short while, asking me certain questions about Spain and our lord, the King. Every day that I was there, I was brought a present of fruit or preserves from him and from the emperor, including some pears, twice as big as the largest you find in Spain.[47]

After I had been at the court six days, the secretary asked me when I would like to see the emperor. I answered that it did not depend on my wishes, but those of His Highness. At this, he left and notified me that the following day, at two o'clock, he would send some gentlemen of the palace to escort me. At that hour, I set out and reached the first gates of the royal palace, where there is not as much to see as in that of his son, nor is the house itself as attractive – although if I had not seen the other I might have thought it so.

There are also other matters in which the prince behaves with greater authority. It is true that in terms of the guards at the gates, and the moats and the walls, there is little difference between the two palaces. The emperor is older and may well fear death, considering the fate of so many of his predecessors. Since these empires are not inherited, but won by tyranny and force of arms, there have by chance been several accidental deaths of kings[48]. For this reason, the emperor lives retired[49] and has more people and armed men about him than the prince. There are also three strong gates as at Yendo, with soldiers at each of them, but in larger numbers than there. Having passed through these, one proceeds to enter the palace apartments. One thing I noticed was that the clothes and insignia of those who received me in each chamber were different from those in the previous one. On reaching the chamber before the one where the emperor sat, his two secretaries came out to meet me. They are the officials who are closest to royal personages in Japan, holding the greatest authority and the most highly esteemed. This is made clear by the large number of attendants who accompany them.

Some time passed in a courteous struggle to decide who would sit in front and in the end they won and set me in the place of honour. The oldest and most eminent of them then made a long speech, congratulating me for having arrived so close to his king, thanks to which all my troubles would find consolation and aid. They, as those ministers who dealt with the most important affairs of the kingdom, would take charge of my concerns and my desires. I thanked them for this and after my reply, the same one continued.

He said that one of the things which had caused the delay was that since the emperor ruled the greatest monarchy in the world, and His Majesty and authority were correspondingly great there could be no dispensing with royal ceremonial. He told me that a great lord might come to see him, one whom they call *dono*, with an income of three million and at more than a hundred paces distance he would be required to bend his knees and bow his head, placing in front of him a rich gift and then return to his lands, without having spoken a word to the emperor and without ever having been addressed in his name. He feared that however much they extended themselves to care for me, I would be surprised at my treatment and accuse the emperor of coldness, although he wished nothing more than to treat me well.

It seemed to me that this warning required me to consider my answer well and so I told the interpreters[50] to listen very carefully to what I said and translate it faithfully. I said that I had paid close attention to the good reasons that he had set forward for me, but that my answer was going to be a repetition for the second time what I had said before.

The King, Don Felipe, my lord, having honoured me by letting me serve him in the government of the Philippines and, while returning to report to him concerning my charge, I would not have come to Japan, for it was many leagues out of my way, but for being driven off course. It was perfectly possible that none of my successors would ever arrive there, except in the case of a similar misfortune. The ship in which I was travelling had been caught in a violent storm and, damaged by the winds and the currents, had run aground on the rocks and reefs off the coast of Japan, where it was broken to pieces. Those who escaped survived by clinging to planks and pieces of wood and we thought that we had reached some desert island. We were then overjoyed to find that it was Japan, where there ruled so great a king and one so clement to strangers.

Naturally, this improved our fate, since clearly for men stripped of everything, whom fortune had cast up there, leaving them nothing but their lives and completely at the mercy of the emperor, any favour shown by him would be most greatly esteemed by me, just as by all the others. I, who for many days had gone by the name of captive, had no cause for complaint at the courtesy that had been done me in granting me my life and showing me so much honour.

But I wished to point out that the Emperor could follow one of two paths in his treatment of me: on the one hand as a private gentleman wrecked in his kingdom, on the other, as the servant of my king and as such a very close representative of his person. In the former case, considered only as myself and in view of what I deserved through my own merits, any favour that His Majesty might show me would more than suffice. However, if it were decided to treat me as the servant and minister of my king, it should be remembered that Don Felipe, my lord, was known as the greatest and most powerful king in all the world, since his kingdom and empires extended throughout the East Indies and the greater part of the New World, not to mention his possessions in Europe, by which his ancestors were considered mighty kings. So, if the Emperor were his friend as he maintained, it seemed to me that His Majesty should try to strengthen and increase this friendship and not risk breaking it by refusing a favour to the subjects and servitors of my king. For myself personally, I assured him, that in whatever way His Highness treated me, I would consider myself much favoured and honoured.

The secretary listened to these words with very great attention and apparent approval and, the interpreter having finished relaying them, he paused for a moment then said that he did not now wish me to enter so promptly to see the Emperor, because what I had said to him seemed of importance and he would go in himself and confer with His Highness. He remained there more than half an hour, which time I spent examining a number of beautiful objects, which the Emperor kept in two niches[51] near where I was waiting, and they were indeed fit for so great a king. The secretary came out and told me that I should enter and that the Emperor was waiting to show me the greatest favour and honour that had ever been shown to anyone in those kingdoms and which would fill their inhabitants with astonishment at such a great innovation. At this point, I proceeded two chambers further on and, although when I had kissed the Prince's hand they had ordered all the servants and people who came with me to stay where they were, here they gave them permission to enter, until they could see the Emperor and they bade them stop and bend their knees to the ground.

The Emperor was in a square room, not very large, but words cannot describe its remarkable beauty. Before me, in the centre, there were several steps going up and where they ended began a grill, all of gold, which went from one side of the room to the other, dividing it a matter of four paces from where the Emperor sat. It was two *varas*[52] high and had many little doors through which servants came and went, for the Emperor called them a number of times, and they were all on their knees with their hands placed on the ground, in the most profound and respectful silence; and on one side and the other, there were some 20 gentlemen. The secretaries and all those who approached the Emperor wore trousers so long that they dragged on the ground more than two palms length, so that no-one by any chance should see their feet[53]. Their cloaks were similar in style and shape to those capes that we have here for going to sporting events[54] with very wide skirts. The Emperor was sitting on a chair of blue velvet and at his left side, some six paces away to the left, another had been placed for me, exactly the same and not different in any way,

The appearance of the Emperor his robes and costume

The robe the Emperor was wearing was azure satin worked with many stars and half moons in silver and his sword was girded on. He wore no hat on his head, but his hair was elaborately braided and tied with coloured ribbons. He is an elderly man, about seventy years old, of medium height, with a venerable yet lively face, not as dark as the prince, but fatter.

I approached him guided by the secretaries and with the reverences and signs of respect that it is the custom in the palace to make to our king. Having been warned not to come too close to him or ask for his hand or kiss it, I remained standing next to the same seat which had been prepared for me, after having made a final reverence as I reached it. Up till then he had not shown any expression, but now he lowered his head a little and smiled at me very affably and lifting his hand made a sign that I should sit down. I made another very low bow and remained standing. He insisted a second time that I should sit, which I did, and then he bade me cover my head.

More time than it takes to say three *Credos* passed in complete silence, then he called the two secretaries who were at his side and ordered them to tell me how happy he was that I had come.

Although troubles and misfortunes could hardly fail to wound my heart, nevertheless I should divert myself and take courage at finding myself in his kingdom, where he would do for me everything that my lord, Don Felipe, would have done for me and even more. I rose and doffed my hat to hear his words and answer him, but he would not let me rise. I said that I kissed his hands for the great kindness he had done me and that the presence of such great kings and monarchs had the power to combat troubles worse than mine. Thus I found myself comforted and I was much cheered and encouraged by being at his court and in the expectation of no less generosity than I would have received at the court of my own king.

After a brief pause, he went on to say that I should consider what I needed in the way of equipment, as well as anything else that might occur to me, and tell his secretaries and it would easily be obtained, as I would see. I answered that the kindness of a king like His Highness was never to be forgotten and that on the following day, I would take advantage of it and tell His Majesty the things that I needed to have. At this point, I wished to rise and take my leave, but he bade me to sit down, saying that he very much enjoyed my visit and he did not want it to be so short and ordered those who wished to see him to enter.

A Japanese Lord visits the Emperor, and his Gift[55]

Next there entered one of the greatest lords of Japan, or so he seemed from his gift, which consisted of ingots of silver and gold and silk garments and other things, to the value of more than twenty thousand ducats. These were first placed on tables and I would not swear that the Emperor even looked at them. Then, more than a hundred paces from where His Highness sat, this *tono* prostrated himself, lowering his head as if he were kissing the ground and no one said a word to him, nor did he raise his eyes to the Emperor, either when he entered or when he took his departure. He then turned to leave with such a great following that, according to some of my servants, three thousand men accompanied him. After him, entered Juan Esquerra[56], the *Capitán General* of my ship who did the same as this lord whom I have just described and in the very same place and then he returned to his house.

A Present from the Governor of the Philippines

Next, the Father Commissary[57], Fray Alonso Muñoz, entered with the present from the Governor of the Philippines[58]. He was favoured with permission to come forward ten or twelve paces, but without a word spoken, he then withdrew like the others. When all this was finished, I asked permission to leave and the Emperor granted it, saying I should go and rest.

His secretaries accompanied me through the first two chambers and then in the same order as I entered, various gentlemen accompanied me, until they left me outside the palace and then others accompanied me to my lodging.

Another day, I went to see Consecundono[59], the Emperor's secretary. Although his house is smaller than the palace, there is no less to see. He came to the last apartments to receive me. He offered me a collation and saluted with the wine, which is very much the custom among them, lifting the cup above his head to toast me. After this, he told me not to waste my time with business but to enjoy what I had, especially since the Emperor was filled with good will towards to me and inclined to favour me. I gave him a document translated into his language and said that to save him trouble, I preferred to tell him the substance of it. I wanted to be brief, but not so brief as to fail to benefit from the Emperor having made me not one promise but three.

Firstly, I begged him that the religious of all the Orders[60] present in Japan might be protected and treated with respect. Also that they should be left freely in their houses and churches without anyone troubling them, because for my Lord, the King Don Felipe, the religious and the ministers of God are the apple of his eye. I made this point the first and most important, because this is the thing over which His Majesty watches most closely.

As my second point, I begged him to maintain and advance the friendship with my Lord the King, Don Felipe. Whatever relationship His Highness might have with any other prince in the world, he would never find one so greatly to his advantage with so great a monarch, nor one so generous or with such noble qualities, and as His Highness came to know him better, although separated by such great distances, he would come to appreciate these qualities the more.

The third request that I wished to make derived from the point I had just made. In order to keep the friendship of my Lord, the King Don Felipe, His Highness should not allow enemies and those in rebellion against his royal crown, as were the Dutch now present his kingdom. I asked him to expel them for even if they were not incompatible with friendship with my king, they were men of evil life and customs and lived as corsairs, roaming the sea. That in itself should be enough to ensure that they do not show their faces before His Highness, nor receive shelter and protection anywhere in his lands, kingdoms and provinces.

The secretary listened to everything that I was requesting and replied that it seemed good to him. He would report it to the Emperor and answer me on the following day. He was so prompt that on the following day at ten o'clock, he was at my lodgings. We went through the exchanges of courtesies in which they are most punctilious and I offered him a collation and there was an exchange of toasts, which is the way they begin more serious matters. Then he told me that, having read my memorial to the Emperor, the latter turned to him full of admiration and said:

"I envy the King, Don Felipe, nothing, except the possession of a retainer such as this. All of you, look and learn. This gentleman was lost at sea and escaped with nothing but his skin. I offered to give him anything he might ask, but he did not ask for gold or silver, or anything for himself, but only what would be useful to his religion and of service to his king. And so, tell him that I will favour him with all he asks and will give orders that henceforth the men of religion who are here in Japan shall not be pursued. In this way, I shall keep the friendship of the King, Don Felipe, and it suits me well to maintain it with so great a king. However, as regards throwing the Dutch out of my kingdom, this year it would be very difficult because they have my word and my safe-conduct, but for the future it goes without saying that I am glad to be warned of their disastrous propensities."

This was how he answered my memorandum, but after he [the secretary] went on and continued as follows:

"The Emperor has told me that I should tell you that he has a good ship[61] and if you need it to travel to New Spain he will order you to be given it, together with sufficient money for your journey."

Also, His Highness has understood that over there mining experts are to be found, who are very competent in the techniques of refining silver and if the king, Don Felipe would send fifty of them, they would be given as great a share as they could want, because although there are vast quantities in these kingdoms[62] at least half is lost through not knowing how to profit from it. I made some difficulties over this, through not knowing the will of my King, but I said that if His Highness would give me permission, I would go to the province of Bungo where the ship, the *Santa Ana*[63], was and if it were not possible to go in her, I would accept the favour of the ship he had offered me. I also said that I would answer him either from there, or by returning to his court, depending on the direction taken over the question of the mining experts.

With this, I took my leave of the court of the Emperor and set off for the province of Bungo. I am now about to tell what happened and what I saw on that journey.

From the city of Surunga and the court of the Emperor, one goes overland to Osaka[64], in order to reach Bungo, passing first through the famous city of Miyako [Kyoto][65]and Fushimi[66], which have on occasion been the residence of the emperors of Japan. From Surunga to Miyako, there are eighty leagues of flat, easy road, although there are some great rivers that are crossed in boats, which are drawn across from one bank to the other. These vessels are so large that they can easily accommodate the passengers' horses, however many may be travelling. One can be quite certain of not having to sleep in any uninhabited place because, as I have mentioned before, in all Japan there is a not a quarter of a league left barren.

If the villages were small, or composed of no more than huts made of branches, it would not be surprising, but I am certain that in no kingdom of the world are to be found so many fine places with so much trade and such beautiful streets and houses. Travelling in this country is most amusing and very pleasant, for on every side there is such an abundance of good things and so many people who come forward to offer them to you almost for nothing. Also, it is not necessary to book lodgings or arrange in advance who will prepare the food, for at any hour of the day, they will bring anything one might ask or want.

Thus I continued on my way to the great city of Miyako (Kyoto), welcomed and entertained along the way by all the governors and gentleman who lived there because the Emperor had warned them of my coming and ordered that it should be so. I am well aware that a very long book could be written on all the towns and villages that I have omitted, for I passed by cities with thirty or forty thousand heads of households, but I don't remember having seen a single village or hamlet on all this journey.

At last, one afternoon, I arrived in sight of the city of Miyako, renowned for the remarkable and outstanding things that are said about it. It lies on a very spacious plain, as was needful for the great multitude of people that inhabit it. I was able to establish that, together with the surrounding area, it has more than eight hundred thousand inhabitants, although some think there are four hundred thousand and others less than three hundred. The truth is that that there is no larger city in any part of the world we know. Its walls stretch ten leagues from one end to the other. I walked from seven in the morning until shortly before prayer[67], only stopping for an hour at midday and even then I had not left behind the first houses.

In this city lives the Daire[68], who is the king of Japan, who is also known by the name of Boy[69]. These kings, since the earliest origins of Japan, have gone on succeeding each other in a direct line. Since the Japanese hold that the majesty of their kings and nobles requires them to be neither seen nor involved in affairs, they always live enclosed. Although by rights and according to the law, he should govern all the kingdoms of Japan, a few years ago Taikosama raised the country in revolt and reduced all the *tonos* and lords to obedience by force of arms.

This Daire, who was the natural king, kept only the name and the right to give out dignities and titles and to invest with honours both the great men of the kingdom and even the Emperor himself. For this purpose, he keeps a special day in the year when all come, each with their individual devices showing their rank. He also bestows ranks and honours on the priests who serve the idols, who are called *bonzos*[70], and he himself is their principal head and high priest. Hence, only the Emperor can excuse himself from attending this ceremony, unless it is on the occasion of his own first investiture, in which case he must perforce appear. In all outward gestures and public ceremonies, the Emperor shows great respect and gives the Daire the place of honour, which is all very fine and good, given the little he subsequently allots him, which is hardly enough for him to live.

The palace and the royal house in which he lives in this city of Miyako is extraordinarily sumptuous and rivals the palaces of the Prince and the Emperor, but I did not see it, for if it is not the special day that I have just mentioned, no one is allowed to see it. He never goes out of his house and, as regards the governing of the city; he has no authority except over that which lies within his own gates.

In this city, there is a viceroy appointed by the Emperor. Although the town of Fushimi is only a league away and Sakai[71] and Osaka are close to the city limits, as well as many other large places, the viceroy of Miyako's jurisdiction does not extend beyond the surrounding canals. Nevertheless, there is as much to be appreciated as in a very large kingdom. He is treated as having the same authority as the Emperor and rarely goes out of his house. He has named six governors for this place alone. He received me and entertained me most generously and asked in great detail about Spanish affairs.

Having spent a considerable time over this, he said that he wanted to repay me for the pleasure he had from what I had told him, by telling me of some of the splendours of the city of which he was viceroy. Although I was filled with admiration and awe, I did not let him see it, because I did not want him to conclude that Spanish cities were inferior. He told me that the city of Miyako alone had five thousand temples to their gods, apart from the many shrines, which did not count. He also told me that there were fifty thousand registered prostitutes in different legally established quarters. He ordered that I should be shown the tomb of Taikosama[72] and the Daybu[73], a metal idol that is there, and the hall of their gods.

These three things took up three different days, because although they are within the city they were so far from my inn that I could not get back there until very late and even then, I was lucky. If a man leaves his house, he needs to be a good pathfinder to get back to it, even if he has gone no more than a short distance.

The Remarkable Size of a Metal Idol in the City of Kyoto.

This idol in metal is called Daybu and could well be one of the Seven Wonders of the World and I don't know that it wouldn't rival the most wonderful of them! It is all of bronze and so large and high that however lavishly one praises it or has it praised to one, it is impossible to imagine what I later saw. Wondering how I could describe it on my return, I sent one of the men who were with me, one of the tallest in all the kingdom, up to measure the size of the right thumb of the idol. He did this in my presence and before more than thirty people, and tried to embrace the thumb with both arms, stretching them out as far as he could, but he needed two palms widths more for his hands to surround it and meet. While it is true that this gives some idea of its size, nothing will describe its proportions, for it is the thing most perfectly finished that has ever been seen. Feet, hands, mouth, eyes, forehead and all the other parts of the face are so fine that if a famous painter were to set out to paint them with the greatest perfection, I do not know if he would achieve what is to be seen there.

They were building the temple when I went there and, according to what has been written to me since, it is still not finished. More than a hundred thousand people, carpenters and craftsmen of all kinds, were involved in the work, which is nothing more than a conduit opened by the devil to persuade the Emperor to waste all the riches of his treasury.

I then went to the burial place of Taikosama and there were innumerable things to see, although it grieves me that such celebrated and sumptuous buildings should have their aim and end the adoration of the ashes of a man whose soul is in hell. The entrance to this temple is by a path that climbs upwards. It is all paved with a kind of white stone with a marbled pattern and, if I am not mistaken, I counted the number of paces and there were four hundred or more. On either side, at intervals of roughly three paces, there were columns of the same stone, five *varas*[74] high and at the top of each a lantern which is lit at nightfall and it is so bright that one hardly misses the day.

At the end of this pathway are the first steps by which one goes up to the temple. Before entering, on the right hand, there is a convent of nuns, who also serve as female chaplains for the services, although in a separate and different place. The principal door by which one enters the temple is entirely marble, with inlays of gold and silver, all different and so elaborately worked that merely by looking at it one can guess what lies within. The main part of the temple rests on pillars and columns of remarkable size and among them a choir with grilles and seats such as we have here in our most famous cathedrals and at the time I visited, chaplains and canons were chanting very much as we are accustomed to do for the Hours. According to what I was told, they also are in the habit of reciting their prayers at prime, terce, vespers and matins[75], but I had qualms about listening to them for I felt I should not pay attention to things so contrary to our holy faith.

The man who was showing me around on the order of the viceroy entered the choir and must have told them who I was, because at that four of the canons came out to receive me. From their clothes, I really would have said that they were some prebends from Toledo, for they looked so like them. Their surplices were no different except that they had very long skirts that took up half of the temple and a kind of biretta very wide a the top and narrow at the bottom. They spoke to me in a very pleasant way and took me to see the altar where his wretched relics are preserved. There is a great multitude of lamps as for the miracles of Our Lady of Guadalupe[76], but the pious and the pilgrims who go there do not number one third as many. I was amazed at this and even more at seeing so many people in the temple, all attending in silence and with the greatest attention and devotion, and I was disconcerted that it should be so very different with us, for we would not be capable of imitating them. They drew back five or six curtains from an iron grill and then others that were of silver and finally the last, which they said was gold. Behind it, in a casket, were the ashes of Taiko. However, no one could see the casket except the high priest, but nevertheless they prostrated themselves on the ground before reaching the last curtain. Just as I remarked their false and deluded devotion, so they must have noticed the lack of respect that I felt for their shrine. To conclude, I got out of there as quickly as possible.

They took me to see their house and their woods and gardens, which could be compared to those of our Lord, the King, at Aranjuez, but although they are equal in terms of the natural beauty of the site and its pleasantness, this owes something more to artifice.

I ate with them that day and they spared no pains to entertain me. From some high galleries, I watched the large numbers of people who visited that house, ceaselessly day and night, according to what they told me, and I noticed that they use holy water – or more correctly, cursed water – and they use rosaries to keep count of their prayers to Jaca and Mida[77], their gods.

Nevertheless, from these they have derived an infinite number of others, so that there are in Japan thirty five different sects and religions, in which some deny the immortality of the soul, others say that there are many gods, others worship the elements, without anyone compelling or forcing them in this matter. So, having gathered all the priests together to petition the Emperor to drive our friars and priests out of Japan, and he, seeing himself hard pressed by them and their arguments, countered: how many different sects and religions do you have in Japan? They answered him: Lord, there are thirty-five. To which he replied very swiftly: Where there are already thirty-five, no matter if there be thirty-six; let them live in peace.

After having been more than two hours in this house, they took me to that of the nuns with which it shares a wall. Their habit consists of blue and white silk dresses and their heads are covered with blue veils – dress more appropriate for a festival than for a convent. The mother superior or abbess came out to receive me in a large chamber and bring me wine and a collation, and she was the first to raise her cup to toast me and with her came the rest of the nuns, some ten or twelve, so that the party would be more complete. They went back in and then came out again with little rattles or bells[78] in their hands and danced for more than half an hour and if they had not been told that it was already time for me to leave, they would not have finished so soon. At which, I said my farewells and returned that evening to my inn.

Another day they took me to see the great house of idols[79] – and it is called "great" with good reason, because it is [the size of] three very wide horse tracks and in it there are 2600 idols, each on its tabernacle, each with its own insignia, depending on what it represents. They are all of gilded metal and the Japanese are pre-eminent in the art of making these figures in metal and it is done with the greatest skill and perfection that can be exhorted of them. A special income is paid to this hall for the worship and upkeep of these idols and I got tired of looking at them, because they were so many, and in them the devil offers these wretched people a yet greater occasion to lose their souls.

In this city of Miyako, there are three monasteries: of the Company, of St Dominic and of St Francis and although the houses and churches are not in full view, but with other buildings in front of them so that they seem like ordinary houses, nevertheless, their presence is very fruitful and there are a great number of Christians.

On the eve of Christmas, I went on from there to Fagime[80], which lies just beyond the outskirts of Miyako. The court sometimes stayed in this city of Fagime until the Emperor moved it to Surunga[81]. Although the streets are somewhat narrow, nevertheless in most aspects it represents the best of Japan. I stopped with the Discalced Fathers [of the Order] of St Francis and it gave me no small joy to see the number of Christians who came to hear and celebrate the holy offices on Christmas night, and almost all took Communion with as many tears and as much devotion as the most deeply earnest men of religion.

From this place I went on to the great city of Osaka[82] by a river like that of Seville, a distance of ten leagues and with just as many ships and as much trade as the other. In some places they tow them and the journey can be made in a day with little trouble. I also stopped in the city of Osaka and this time again I lodged in the house of the Fathers of St Francis; those of the Company and of St Dominic are also established there. In my opinion, this place is the most beautiful in all Japan. It has 200,000 inhabitants and since the sea beats against the very houses, it enjoys in the greatest abundance the fruits of both sea and land. The houses as a rule are two stories high and worked in a remarkable way.

The city of Sacay is right next door, two leagues away and although I did not see it, I know that it has more than 80,000 inhabitants. I embarked at Osaka on a ship that they call *junca*, about the size of those that go along the river at Seville. I set out for the province of Bungo[83], which is also the route to Nagasaki[84] where there is a bishop and some Portuguese, and it is where the martyrdom of those holy martyrs took place.

Although the journey takes 12 or 15 days by sea, one sleeps almost every night on land and it is very rare to lose any of the ships. We passed very beautiful places, although not as heavily populated as those that lay behind. Having reached Bungo, a few days later the burning of that unfortunate Macao galleon[85] took place on the orders of the Emperor and on account of the rebelliousness of the commander[86] in charge of it. He had summoned him twice and ordered him to come to his court to answer the charge that he had hung some Japanese in Macao with very little reason, among them two ambassadors whom the Emperor was sending to the kingdom of Siam[87] and who had put in there because of the tempests. The captain said he did not want to go into the presence and seeing this lack of respect, the Emperor gave the order that he should be arrested and the galleon should either be sent to the bottom or burned. The Japanese chose the latter and carried it out with such determination that they stormed it with artillery and set fire to the poop, so that none escaped of those who were in her. This action on the part of the Emperor was justified, since hanging his vassals and ambassadors did not seem prudent behaviour, in view of the friendship with our lord the King, and I did not approve of it. But as I had spoken in court on behalf of the captain, he ordered his secretary to write down for me the true reason he had had for doing what he did.

And so for this matter, as well as the question of mining engineers and mines, and also the question of the Dutch, he wanted me to return and he also wanted to know whether I wished to go to New Spain in his ship. Father Luìs Sotelo, a friar of the Order of St Francis, who had brought some of my letters from Miyako, had begun to arrange this. The captain of the *Santa Ana* had indeed offered me his ship, but it had spent thirteen days run aground and was very old and unsafe, and also I was in the middle of very important negotiations with the Emperor on behalf of our lord the King, as an essential link in this capitulation. This and the other clauses are today before the council, together with the *chapas*[88] and royal decrees that the Emperor gave me. I am going to give a brief account of these matters and it is the truth that I never claimed anything other than to take the right direction and path towards spiritual well-being and the conversion of those souls and, in second place, to re-establish the friendship of the Emperor with His Majesty and expel the Dutch from there.

The Clauses and Conditions that Don Roderigo Requested of the Emperor

In response to the clause concerning the fifty mining experts whom the Emperor requested, I said that I would be responsible for suggesting it to His Majesty and to his Viceroy in New Spain, but in order to make it more certain and to facilitate matters, His Highness the Emperor should concede the following things to me:

That these miners should be given half [the profits] of the mines where they are working and extracting the metal, and the other half should be divided into two parts, one for my lord the King, Don Felipe, and the other for His Highness the Emperor. As regards the part pertaining to my lord the King, he should have factors and agents in Japan and they should be able to have with them priests of whichever of the Orders they prefer, with public places of worship and churches to celebrate the Divine Offices, and although these were the last words of this clause of the agreement, the first thought and principal aim was directed towards this end, and so likewise with the others that follow.

Then I think I said that since His Highness the Emperor had a firm friendship with my lord the King, as it is right that kings should have between them, which cannot be broken without breaking the bond of their promises, and since it is impossible to have two enemies in one house, I said that His Highness should give orders that the Dutch should leave his kingdom, for otherwise neither the King, my lord, nor his ships would ever be able to guard their backs in Japan.

After this clause, I requested in another that if any of the ships of my lord the King, Don Felipe, arrived in Japan, either forced to land, or because it was their destination, then the Emperor should have them given safe harbour and also safe-conduct, so that no-one could do them harm or damage, nor seize their merchandise, but that they should be protected and favoured as if they were really vessels or ships belonging to His Highness.

The third clause said that in case the King, Don Felipe, my lord wanted to build ships or galleys[89] to send to the Moluccas or Manila and needed help as regards supplies, provisions and munitions in order to support the forces there, that His Majesty should order that craftsmen be made available for this work and that supplies, provisions, ropes, anchors and munitions for these ships and those sailing for New Spain should be provided at the prices current in the kingdom. Again, that permission should be given for any shipyard or shipyards that the King, Don Felipe, my lord should wish to establish for this purpose, and that his agents should be allowed to have with them priests to say Mass for them and churches where the Divine Offices could be celebrated.

I remember that I also asked that whenever His Majesty sent a captain or ambassador that he should always be received in all the kingdoms of Japan and lodged as befitted a person who came in the name of so great a king, and that he himself could also bring priests and ministers to say Mass for him and keep public churches for that purpose. He would have authority over all the Spaniards who might be in Japan and punish them if they committed any crime.

These are the capitulations, more or less as I remember them that Father Luìs Sotelo took. The Emperor conceded all of them and opened the ports throughout the kingdom. Only the question of the Dutch remained unresolved, for he never took any further decision in that matter beyond the first, when he answered me that he had given them his word. As regards the mining experts, he said that it remained to be seen and that there was no definite promise, but depending on their skill and the silver they extracted, he would do what I asked and much more if it seemed appropriate and that he would consider the matter again and perhaps come to a decision before my departure.

Considering that it was of service to His Majesty to bring these matters to a conclusion and to see whether I could extirpate this root which was beginning to take hold in Japan, in other words the Dutch, it seemed to me the lesser evil was to risk remaining there some years, rather than giving reason for it to be said that for my own convenience and in order to set sail, I had abandoned such important matters begun and set in motion. And if the clause relating to the silver, which I had asked very privately should be granted, as I had hopes it would be shortly, it is the most certain truth that it would be worth more than a million to the King, my lord.

And so I prepared to return to the Court of the Emperor, which I did by the same route and stages by which I had come. There, I was very well received and remained for several months during which time they prepared the *chapas* and the royal ordinances granting all the clauses that I have mentioned, except for the two relating to the Dutch and the silver, where there was nothing new. And as a sure gage of the friendship that the Emperor wished to establish once again with the King, my lord, he agreed to send an ambassador and a gift, and another for the Viceroy, choosing for this purpose a Friar of St Francis, or some other Order, as I saw fit. I named Fray Alonso Muñoz[90] and he gave him six decrees and the license to depart, although he wanted me to have both the former and the present one myself.

He also lent me his ship and 4,000 ducats of Castile in order to furnish what was needful and, if it seemed opportune, to sell it there, and that I should send him the proceeds in merchandise. After doing me all these favours, the Emperor allowed me to leave his Court and sent me to that of the prince, his son, who also wrote to the King, our lord and sent a present and another for the Viceroy. It was there that the preparations were made for the departure of the ship, the *San Buenaventura*, in which I came and they gave me everything necessary, so that I could set out on the 1st of August in the year 1610 and I reached the port of Matanchel[91] at the mouth of the Californias on the 26th of October in the same year, after the happiest and most fortunate voyage that has ever been known in the Southern Sea.

What remains for me to say at the end of this account is what I have already reported: the furthest headland of Japan which was drawn in at 33 ½° is in fact at 35½° on a level with Yubanda where I was wrecked, and this is the true extremity of Japan. Nevertheless the Emperor has vassals who recognize him and pay him tribute in the interior of the country, as far as 46° latitude and beyond. This is what the English pilot[92] told me, who was wrecked there and has been resident in Japan for more than twelve years. He is a very great cosmographer and mathematician and the Emperor, in order to learn something of this science, to which he is much inclined, has shown him great grace and favour. And he told me that he sent him to collect some property taxes[93]and that he took with him his astrolabe which gave a reading of 45° – and he had not advanced as far as he could have done.

Japan has an infinity of islands and they almost touch each other. Great China is 200 leagues from Japan and Korea is 50 leagues beyond the last Japanese island. Japan has 66 subject kingdoms and provinces and the kingdom of Korea is next to China and is very rich and prosperous. The Emperor Taikosama conquered Korea, having sent 150,000 Japanese, but the Emperor having died they loosed their hold on it and did not know or even want to keep what they had won, for although the land was so good, their own seemed better to them. The people of Korea are not warlike and enjoy the same wealth and abundance as Japan and China. Some such undertaking [i.e. war] might be attempted in order to display the friendship of the Emperor with the King our lord. Although no door is open in Japan, except that of the Holy Gospel, in Korea by that means and by that of arms, the hopes of His Majesty could be much strengthened, based first of all on the Emperor of Japan, without whose support this could neither be undertaken nor even considered.

The Japanese are far braver and more warlike than the Chinese, or the people of Ternate[94], or any of the surrounding countries. In Manila they use arquebuses skilfully and take accurate aim, but are not swift. They have some pieces of artillery, but few and they handle them badly. They are extremely obedient in warfare, but at the moment they are not at war with anyone and I don't know with whom they could be. Even if the Great Chinaman[95] were to risk his power, there are places in Japan that nature has made impregnable. The heavens have endowed this region with singular advantages. The weather is like that of Spain, although the winter is very much colder. They know nothing of famine or plague, indeed have never heard tell of them and those who have the worst time there are the poor, because of their oppression by the rich whom they are forced to serve. However, the abundance of grain that they harvest, without there ever being a bad year for wheat, barley and rice, sustains them all comfortably. Indeed, they want foreigners to come and ships that will carry away the provisions, as they send them to Manila with good returns and profit.

The Japanese have the vice of drinking, which leads to other greater evils, since they are not satisfied with their women, sometimes more than a hundred of them, but they try to have as many as possible. And although they are not faithful, for the women it is the reverse, indeed it is something very rare and noteworthy for a married woman to betray her husband. The Japanese are extremely quick-witted, but not at all constant or reliable. They are famous merchants and greatly admire whoever cheats the most in this business. In Japan today, there are more than 300,000 Christians, among all of whom, as with us, the hope that our holy Catholic Faith will spread and grow strong is very great. May God grant them their aim, as He can and as is fitting for His greater glory.

It seems to me clear that if the ships from Manila broke their journey to New Spain by stopping in a Japanese port, the journey would be safer and would present fewer risks to the health of all the travelers, for one of the causes of losses is that these ships set out from Manila loaded up to the sails and this overloading is not due to the cargo but to the essential stores of provisions. If it were possible to carry only what was needed to reach Japan and there take on what was required to continue to New Spain, the boats would be lighter on departure and provisioning would take place in a cold climate, where food-stuffs are cheaper and keep better and would be better for the health, for their putrefaction is one of the main causes of the death of so many people. In this way, the voyages would have better chance of success.

One can cite the example of the three ships that left Japan and enjoyed a most fortunate crossing. Additional undeniable reasons are as follows: the optimal route for the ships setting out from Manila and the one which has given the best results is that which heads swiftly to a higher latitude, avoiding the Islas de los Ladrones[96], where hurricanes and tempests put ships in a great predicament, and in addition the higher latitude brings one closer to Japan. Furthermore, it follows that if the junks and light Japanese boats setting sail from Manila are never wrecked, unless they leave too late in the season, and arrive in 15 or 20 days, this voyage should be all the better for our boats which are stronger and manned by more expert pilots and seamen. Heading out straight for Japan, there are a thousand safe ports, for they all are, as is the whole of the coast in the months of June, July and August, which is their summer. And if Your Majesty intends to settle Rica de Plata[97], which is a hundred and fifty leagues from the furthermost point of Japan, so that the Manila ships can repair the damage done by the storms that habitually rage in those parts, it is clear that they can best achieve these ends the closer they are to where the damage takes place. Also, where they can easily find provisions and water, and where rope is virtually for free, as well as anchors and things made of iron and wood, and where there are not only craftsmen to repair ships, but also to build them. Nothing like that, or anything as suitable, is to be found in Biscay or Seville.

Among the advantages that would follow from Your Majesty's friendship with the Emperor, the aforementioned is one; but it must be said that there are various opinions on this, even among the pilots themselves. Thus, I would not make it a general rule, but rather that each should take advantage of this opportunity, as best it seems to him.

The aid that our lord the King sends to the Moluccas by way of provisions, materiel and munitions, as well as some ships, all comes from the Philippines at great expense to the Treasury and for these islands and their inhabitants it is the most vexing burden imaginable. When in one year I had to requisition 10,000 baskets of rice in the provinces of Oton and Cebu, even paying for it at a good price, I was afraid that the Indians of the region would revolt, and for fear of this, I fortified these places, as well as their frontiers. The cost of constructing galleys and ships in the Philippines is equally intolerable, for there is little wood and it is at the price of their own blood that the Indians drag it out using only manpower, to their great prejudice and displeasure.

The iron brought from Japan is clearly cheaper in the country itself and, while sailing from Manila to the Moluccas takes two months and is not safe, it is possible to go from Japan in 20 days without any difficulty. Furthermore, supplies can be bought in Japan for almost nothing and the same is true of munitions and equipment. As regards the building of galleys and other vessels, it will all be done so differently that Your Majesty will save three fourths [of the cost]. There is therefore nothing further to discuss as regards this clause, since everything would be cheaper and better. It will also save the Philippines a burden so heavy that it weighs upon the conscience, as well as shortening the journey and ensuring that nothing will be lacking.

There are different views as to the desirable consequences – in the service of God and our King – of opening up trade between Japan and New Spain, and what advantages would accrue to us from this route. It is certainly true that Japan does not have useful goods to send to New Spain in return, since paintings, writing desks and the things that were brought on the previous occasion are not everyday trade items. For this same reason, if New Spain sends useless and superfluous goods, such as cloth, indigo, cochineal, skins, braids, felt, hats, serge, *guergitas*[98] and wine and receive in exchange silver and gold, which are so abundant there and so much needed here, the opposing view based on the argument that Japanese goods are not needed in New Spain loses its force. Furthermore, Your Majesty will be spared no small expense by bringing anchors, cables, sails and cordage from Japan at the very low prices current there. Manila sends to Japan what it has to export to Mexico: the profits are great, and this is a matter of some interest. This has all been said with no intention other than to choose the best path in the service of God and our lord the King.

Notes

1 In fact 1609 – clearly a slip, perhaps of the copyist, since Vivero gives the date correctly elsewhere.
2 The name commonly given at this date to Cape Nojima at the southern tip of the Boso Peninsula, separating Tokyo Bay from the open Pacific.
3 On the rising of the Japanese at Dilao outside Manila and Vivero's part in the sequel, see Introduction and also de Morga.
4 In fact Tokugawa Ieyasu – see Introduction for this confusion and political situation in Japan at this date.
5 Modern Iwawada on the Bosu Peninsula.
6 A Spanish league is often given as the rough equivalent of 5½ km (c.3½ miles)
7 Feudal lord – *tono* is pronounced, and sometimes written, *dono*.
8 JM suggests that Vivero combined the name of the Honda family, who were lords of the region with Otaki, the main town.
9 *Quimones* – lined, but perhaps also padded or quilted, as autumn was drawing on.
10 *Dairo* or *daire* designates *tenno heika* – the Emperor – but Vivero regularly confuses the Emperor with the Shogun.
11 *Naginata* – an elegant halberd type weapon, used for attacking cavalry, with a wooden shaft and curved blade. In feudal times, women on occasion trained in its use for self-defence in their lord's absence; at later periods, it was associated with Buddhist warrior monks, or *sohei*.
12 Across much of the Far East, the left side is associated with *yang* the masculine principle and is considered to take precedence over the right.
13 *Cathana*. Slightly curved single-edged sword, particularly associated with the samurai. The term has gone into Portuguese as *catana* and is used for large knife or machete.
14 Tokugawa Hidetada
15 Yendo, Yedo or Edo, was the capital of the Tokugawa shogunate from 1603. In 1868, it was renamed Tokyo.
16 Surunga or Sunpu, now part of Shizuoka City, was among the fiefs of the Tokugawa family. Tokugawa Ieyasu (1543-1616) spent his childhood there as a hostage and retired there when he nominally handed over power to his son, Tokugawa Hidetada in 1605. Their relations had been strained since the Battle of Sekigahara in 1600.
17 Vivero – in common with many Spanish writers – confuses the emperor and the shogun and calls the retired shogun, Tokugawa Ieyasu (see n.16) "emperor" throughout. The emperor at this date was in fact Go-Yozei (1586-1611).
18 There is some debate as to the origin of the word *chapa* (probably from the

Hindi rather than the Portuguese), in English, chop – see Hobson-Jobson, on-line at www.bibliomania.com – but the original meaning seems to have been the seal or the stamped travel permits of the shogunate: paper with a square red seal known as *shuin-jo* – red seal or *go-shuin*.

19 This was not peculiar to Japan: the same was permitted in Europe and New Spain under maritime law – *ius littoris* or *ius naufragii* (see *The Japanese in the Philippines*).

20 Otaki in Chiba Prefecture has roughly the same population today. The castle was reconstructed in modern materials in the 1970s and the town is twinned with Cuernavaca in Mexico.

21 1 *estado* = c.1.60m, therefore this moat would be about 80m /c.262 feet deep, which seems unlikely. Vivero may have been confused by the steep gradient of the hillside.

22 In Central America today, a *vara* is 33" or 84cm, giving the wall a height/width of c.5m or c.16 ½ feet.

23 Tokaido – "East Sea Route" – one of the five major roads leading to Yendo or Edo [Tokyo] established by Tokugawa Ieyasu from 1601, in order to consolidate his control over the country.

24 The Shogunate was officially established in Edo on March 24th, 1603 and the city grew at an impressive rate. When residence in the capital for part of the year was imposed in the 1630s, the population was estimated at c.430,000, growing to over a million by the early 18th century (Chandler – see Bibl.).

25 The name Edo means literally "bay door", i.e. estuary, and it is easy to forget today the vital role played in its development by water. The city evolved from a fishing village and the Sumida River was once its main artery.

26 A small coin, 1/16th of a *real* or "piece of eight", at this date roughly 1/16th of an ounce of silver. It is difficult to calculate the value of coins in the past in terms of their purchasing power, especially when several countries are involved. Based on the value of the silver, it could approximate to c.50 US cents or 30 UK pence.

27 Bread – *pan* – was introduced into Japan by the Portuguese in the mid-16th century and the word comes from the Portuguese *pão*.

28 Vivero uses term *portales*, which in Mexico means "portico" or "arcade", perhaps referring to the overhanging roofs along typical Edo streets, at least at a later date.

29 *Labancos* – a type of South American duck.

30 Prostitution was extremely common in Japan, but under the Shogunate efforts were made, as with other aspects of Japanese life, to control it, for political rather than moral reasons. Tokugawa Hidetada restricted the trade to designated quarters of the major cities. The Edo [Tokyo] red-light district of Yoshiwara was established in 1617.

31 The Venetian *ducat* – c.3.5gr of gold – had been a major trade currency across Europe and into Asia since the late 13thc. By the time of Vivero, however, the Spanish coinage was beginning to take its place. Based on the price of gold today, 20,000 ducats would equal c. £1,700,000, which is probably too high.

32 Vivero confuses shogun and emperor throughout the following text.

33 Even then there was a slight squeamishness about eating meat: for example wild boar was known as *yamanokujira* – "mountain whale" – while rabbits

and hares were sometimes classified as birds, so that eating them was a less serious sin.

34 At this date the Franciscans claimed to have ten monasteries and seven hospitals in Japan mostly in the Kanto region.

35 Mukai Shōgen (c.1581-1641), Admiral of the Fleet under Tokugawa Ieyasu, whom he strongly encouraged to promote trade contacts with Mexico. He was partly responsible for the construction of the boat that took the Japanese mission to Mexico in 1614. According to Richard Cocks, Mukai Shōgen discussed the possibility of an invasion of the Philippines with Will Adams and himself in 1616.

36 Spanish attempt at rendering Kozuke-no-Suke dono, one of the titles of Honda Masazumi, minister of the Tokugawa shogunate.

37 By slightly after this date, Edo Castle – Chiyoda-jō – had a perimeter of 16km. The present Imperial Palace stands on part of the site.

38 See Introduction.

39 See n.22 c. 3.36m or 11′.

40 The numbers that fought on the Tokugawa side at the decisive Battle of Sekigahara in 1600 have been variously estimated, upwards of 80,000, which means that Vivero's impression need not be a wild exaggeration.

41 *Tatames*

42 Hidetada (1579-1632) would have been 29.

43 Vivero's word is *vezinos*, used at that date to mean "heads of households", not "neighbours"which gives figures on the high side, since the number is usually multiplied by five or six to give a rough estimate of the population.

44 Meaco – Miyako, i.e."the capital", modern Kyoto.

45 Vivero's word is *corillo*. At a later date, the Tokaido markers, as they appear for example in Hiroshige's 28th Station, were about 10 foot high and square and were often earthen mounds, which marked out distances roughly every 2.4 miles.

46 *Taiko* – retired regent or chief adviser – with the honorific *sama* was the title given to Ieyasu's predecessor, Toyotomi Hideyoshi, the man largely responsible for the unification of Japan. It may have been used to Vivero, referring to Ieyasu, or there may have been some misunderstanding.

47 The large, crisp, scented Japanese *nashi* (Pyrus pirifolia) is still considered a very suitable seasonal gift.

48 Notably Oda Nobunaga (1534-1582). Both Toyotomi Hideyoshi and Tokugawa Ieyasu were his followers, but it is unlikely that it would have been thought suitable to tell Vivero the story of his suicide (*seppuku*), which may explain the rather odd phrase of "muertes accidentales".

49 See Introduction: *The Political Situation in Japan* for the system of *insei* – retired emperors – being adopted by the early shoguns.

50 See section XLIV of *Advice*. The interpreters were two Jesuit priests, one being the Italian, Father Giovanni Battista Porro.

51 Perhaps *tokonoma*: the traditional alcove for displaying selected treasures.

52 c.66″ or 168cm

53 These trousers would have been *naga-hakama* covering the feet and trailing behind. They were required wear for the samurai on court occasions, because they impeded walking and so made an assassination attempt more difficult.

54 *Torneos* – clearly not "jousts" at this date. Perhaps bull-fights?

55 These headings were written in the margin [JM].

56 The very elderly Capitán General de la Armada, or person in charge of the defence of the convoy of ships in the Carrera de Indias, about whom Vivero complained: see section XLIV of *Advice*. Also www.gutenberg.org The Project Gutenberg eBook of The Philippine Islands, 1493-1898: Volume XVII, 1609-1616, for documents relating to him.

57 Of Japan. Fray Alonso was acting as the Shogun's envoy on account of the illness of Fray Luis Sotelo.

58 According to de Morga p.197, Pedro de Acuña had sent the following presents a few years earlier: " …a very large and valuable Venetian mirror, some glass-ware, Castilian clothes, honey, some large China jars and other things known to be pleasing to the Daifu." See also JM note 44.

59 Whom, presumably, he had already met – see note 32

60 Jesuits, Franciscans, Dominicans and Augustinians.

61 Built by William Adams.

62 The great mines of Iwami Ginzan (active 1526-1923 and, since 2007, a UNESCO World Heritage Site) are calculated to have produced a third of the world's silver during the 16th century and to have rivalled Potosí. The cupellation technique *(haifuki-ho)* was introduced from Korea in 1533, but the mercury amalgamation technique seems not to have reached Asia. It was known in the Islamic world in the Middle Ages, and was rediscovered in South America in 1571, perhaps in part through knowledge inherited from Muslim technicians in al-Andalus. See also Introduction: *Silver and Silver Mining*.

63 Travelling with the *San Francisco*, the *Santa Ana* was wrecked on the way to Acapulco.

64 Usaca – Toyotomi Hideyoshi's spectacular castle was begun in 1583. His son, Hideyori, had been defeated by Tokugawa Ieyasu at the battle of Sekigara in 1600, but at this date Hideyori still held Osaka.

65 Meaco. See note 39. Miyako or Kyoto of course was still the residence of the Emperor. See Introduction.

66 Fujime, now a ward of Kyoto.

67 Presumably the *Angelus*, traditionally said at 6.00 a.m., noon and 6.00 p.m.

68 See note 10.

69 The Emperor at that date was Go-Yozei. It has not been possible to establish what Vivero intended.

70 From the Japanese *bonsō* – a Buddhist monk; c.p. obsolete English *bonze*.

71 *Sacay*, now a suburb of Osaka, was one of the most important ports in Japan from medieval times and at this date one of the richest cities, a centre of manufacturing firearms and the arms trade.

72 Toyokuni Jinja in Kyoto's eastern hills – Higashiyama-ku – was a Shinto shrine built in 1599 to honour Toyotomi Hideyoshi, who was revered as a *kami*, or ancestral spirit. The shrine was demolished by Tokugawa Ieyasu in 1615 and rebuilt by the Meiji Emperor in 1868.

73 The Kyoto Daibutsu – Great Buddha – had a turbulent history. Standing roughly on the site of the Kyoto National Museum, it was commissioned by Toyotomi Hideyoshi as a political statement to rival the great Buddha at Nara. It measured 48m high and the metal came from the swords confiscated

in the course of disarming the non-samurai population. Image and hall (Daibutsu-den) were destroyed in the earthquake of 1596 and replaced by a wooden image, which was destroyed by fire in 1602. In 1610, Toyotomi Hideyori decided to replace both image and temple (Hoko-ji). This was presumably what Vivero saw, in which case work must have been completed earlier than date usually given. This statue was destroyed in the earthquake of 1662, although it was presumably restored again, since it was described by Engelbert Kaemfer, who was in Japan 1690-2. What survives of Hoko-ji has been incorporated into the older Shokoku-ji in northern Kyoto. The last Daibutsu is alleged to have been broken up in the Edo period to provide metal for coins. See Engelbert Kaempfer, *History of Japan*, tr. from the original manuscript by John Scheuchzer, London, 1727.

74 Roughly 4m.20cm or 13'9".

75 *Prime*: 6.00 a.m.; *terce*: 9.00 a.m., matins: dawn prayer; vespers: sunset or evening prayer.

76 In the early 14th century, the Virgin Mary appeared to a shepherd at Guadalupe in Spain and her shrine became a much visited rallying point for the Reconquista. In 1531, She appeared to a Mexican Indian, Juan Diego, now a saint, near Mexico City. Her image miraculously transferred to his cloak was identified with the Virgin of Guadalupe. Chosen as Patroness of Mexico and of the Americas, She was credited with many miracles and Her shrine is now the second most visited in the world. Vivero was probably thinking of the Mexican Guadalupe.

77 From the names given to the Buddha: Shaka Nyorai or Sakyamuni and Amida Butsu, the form in which he is principally worshipped by the Pure Land sect.

78 Perhaps *kagura suzu*, the clusters of small bells used in Shinto ritual dance. The Jesuit, Father Pedro Chirino, also mentions the Japanese Christians dancing in church before the Sacrament: "The Japanese who came to Manila also repaired to our church; and once saw them perform a very decorous and devout dance in a feast of the most holy sacrament. Their mode of dress is decorous, and they sing, to a low and solemn music, marking the pauses by strokes with a small fan grasped in the palm of the left hand; they move in time with this, only stamping their feet, inclining their bodies somewhat. The effect is most striking, and invites devotion, especially in those who understand what they sing, which are all things pertaining to the divine." *Relación de la Islas Filipinas*, Roma, 1604. p.200 and at www.gutenberg.org *The Philippine Islands, 1493-1898*: Volume XII, 1601-1604.

79 JM suggests that this is Sanjusangendo – the Hall of the Thirty Three Spaces – which seems plausible. Rebuilt in 1266 after a fire, it contains more than 1,000 statues standing on lotus pedestals. They are in fact of gilded wood, not metal.

80 Probably Fushimi. Toyotomi Hideyoshi built a castle at Fushimi, Momoyama-jō (Peach Mountain Castle) 1592-4 and it was most luxuriously decorated. His intention was to hold peace talks there with Chinese envoys to resolve the war in Korea, but the castle was damaged in an earthquake. It was rebuilt, however, and finally demolished in 1623.

81 Modern Shizuoka. This branch of the official Tokaido dates from 1619 – see also n.23.

82 Usaka.
83 Old name for a province of eastern Kyushu, looking towards Shikoku and Honshu.
84 Nangazaque. Nagasaki was the most Catholic city in Japan and there, on February 5th, 1597, 26 Christians, 20 of whom were Japanese, were crucified. The "Great Martyrdom" of Nagasaki took place in 1622.
85 *Nossa Senhora de Graça.* See Introduction – *Christianity in Japan and the Political Situation.*
86 *Capitán mayor*
87 See Introduction – *The Japanese in South East Asia*
88 *Chapa* – there is some discussion about the origins of this. In Spanish and Portuguese it means a metal plate – for example in modern usage a police badge. In India it was used for an official document or permit engraved on metal, as being more difficult to falsify, or sometimes a seal.
89 *Naos y galeras.*
90 Almost nothing seems to be known about him.
91 The Manila galleons frequently halted there on the coast of Mexico, not far from modern San Blas and at the mouth of the Gulf of California, before reaching Acapulco .
92 Will Adams
93 *Derechos reales*
94 One of the Spice Islands in the Moluccas (Maluku) in Eastern Indonesia, where St Francis Xavier spent part of 1546-7. In 1606, the Spaniards had conquered a Portuguese fortress there and deported the Sultan of Ternate. Half a century later, however, they lost out to the Dutch.
95 "El Gran Chino" – the Wanli Emperor (1563-1620) of the Ming.
96 "Islands of Thieves" – the Marianas.
97 The islands "Rich in Gold and Silver", were in fact legendary, but nevertheless a number of expeditions were inspired to search for them.
98 *Rajas* – serge; *guergitas* – a type of cloth, unidentified.

Advice and Plans[1]

Note on Vivero's *Advice and Plans*

Only some sections of Vivero's *Advice* survive, as his grandson tells us in a note following Ch.XLVI. Although they are all of interest, and Vivero's suggestions were often sound, they must have offended a large number of his contemporaries, especially at the court at Madrid, and may explain why he never received the highest honours, to which he clearly felt entitled. Here, only the sections dealing with Japan and the Philippines have been translated. The information overlaps to some extent with the main narrative, but there are enough differences for it to seem worthwhile including them.

Contents

sure wrongs are checked, and everyone will thus fear to break the royal commands.

X – Which shows how another effective policy could be instituted so that His Majesty does not have to keep his sword permanently unsheathed.

XI – The reasons that exist for the poverty of Spain and the importance of the wealth of the subjects in order for the King to be wealthy; and that the number of universities should be curbed.

XII – XXVI – Already lost at the time of Vivero's grandson – see the paragraph at the end of Ch.XLVI of the *Avisos*

XXVII – That people should not be allowed to leave Spain for the Indies, for the country is rapidly being stripped of its population.

XXVIII – That coaches should be forbidden or their use moderated.

XXIX – That having so many meetings on so many subjects should be avoided and similarly having present at them people of completely irrelevant professions.

XXX – That the Casa de Contratazion[6] in Seville should have a president experienced in arms[7] and one who has sailed to the Indes.

XXXI – That the expenses and outgoings for the Real Hazienda[8] should be reduced for the following items.

XXXII – That there should be shipyards, and that gunpowder should be manufactured in great quantities.

XXXIII – On shipbuilding in the Southern Sea.

XXXIV – On the discovery of the Philippines – their importance and problems.

XXXV – On the importance of preserving the Indians and looking after them, for they are in the process of vanishing and once they are gone, there are no Indies.

XXXVI – On how Spain impoverishes the Indies and the Indies enrich Spain and how important it is that foreigners should not go there and that those who are there should be expelled.

XXXVII – On the great importance of preventing the establishment of colonies in Virginia from the very beginning[9], as well as that which has been set up in Bermuda, for everywhere they have ships, shipyards and foundries.

XXXVIII – That the best solution for the [defence of] the coasts of Spain would be to entrust them to the Military Orders[10].

XXXIX – On what has been discussed in Council regarding the transport of silver from Peru by way of the *desaguadero* of Nicaragua[11]; its pros and cons and what the author has seen of the matter.

XL – In case it should be deemed fitting to move the trade routes so that they pass through the province of Panama and the *desaguadero* of Granada[12]; Panama should not be dismantled, in order to prevent some enemy occupying the empty space and making themselves masters of the two seas.

XLI – On the importance of sending 1,000 blacks each year to New Spain and the losses to the Royal Fifth of not doing so.[13]

XLII – On the importance of carrying out the royal decrees and ordenances and that the public prosecutors[14] should take greater care over this, for it is a shame that, everything having been prepared, all should be wasted through failure of execution.

XLIII – That as regards the government, *encomiendas*[15]and positions of honour of the Indies, preference should be given first of all to those born there and the descendants of those who won that very land, for those men are by no means undeserving, and there have been among them men most outstanding in letters, arms and government.

XLIV – On the refinement of its places and kingdoms and the splendid possessions held by this king [of Japan].

XLV – Continuing on the subject of the Japanese, their marriages and the way that they treat their women and that they do not have the custom of dowries – a practice that would not be at all bad for Spain.

XLVI – On the difference in character between the Japanese and the Chinese; the Japanese priding themselves on being fierce and courageous, the Chinese on being gentle, moderate and long-suffering, and on the great restraint of the Chinese, following the example of their king, as regards the favours which the lords and great men distribute.

Notes

1   *Abisos y Proyectos*
2   These were high tribunals to which all of criminal and civil sentences in a given territory could be sent for appeal. They were modeled, in the Indies, on the Real Audiencias y Chancillerías of Valladolid and Granada. In the territories

where no Viceroyalty existed, such as in the Caribbean, they also exercised supreme administrative and political authority, and were subordinate only to the Consejo de Indias in Spain.

3   Vivero himself had been involved in running the mines in New Spain.
4   Discovered by Juan de Bermúdez in 1503, but the Spanish made no effort to colonize it. In 1607 an English ship ran aground there – Shakespeare's play *The Tempest* is thought to have been inspired by accounts of the experience – and James I decided to claim it. Settlement began in 1612. Vivero had long been exhorting the Crown to check English colonization in both Virginia and the Caribbean – discussed in section xxxvii – on the grounds that the settlements would provide bases for pirates attacking the Spanish treasure fleets and challenge the Spanish presence in what are now Florida, California, New Mexico and along the Oregon Coast.
5   An Indian people in Western Panama, many of whom retreated to the mountains to avoid contact with the Spanish.
6   The Casa de Contratación was the government agency that controlled Spanish colonial affairs, exploration as well as trade.
7   *de capa y espada*
8   Real Hacienda – Exchequer
9   Jamestown was founded by Sir Walter Raleigh in 1607.
10 The Military Orders, combining religious vows with military training, were of great importance in Spain, originally forged to protect the Christians and drive out the Muslim invaders. The most important by this date were the knights of St John, Alcántara and Santiago.
11 Río San Juan de Nicaragua which runs along the border with Costa Rica, emerging into the Caribbean. It was of great importance before the construction of the Panama canal.
12 Called the *desaguadero* of Nicaragua in the previous section.
13 For use in the mines. *The quinto real* was the 20% of any treasure, mined or captured, payable to the king. A lack of slaves would, clearly, have affected the amount of precious metals extracted. Vivero felt strongly that it was cruel and wasteful to use Indians in the mines, since they were not strong enough for the work and had many skills that could be put to better use.
14 *fiscales*
15 Control over land, granted to settlers in the Indies, generally for a specified number of generations.

Ch III

On the [form of] government of the Japanese and Chinese and in particular what the author learned when he was shipwrecked there in the year 1609

Not wishing to cut the thread on the subject of government, I shall say what I learned while governing the Philippines of the customs of the kings of China, and later in Japan, where I was a captive in the year 1609 – although afterwards I was much favoured and shown great honours by the Emperor. I knew that they shared the same [customs] and although these two nations dislike each other and are opposed, their form of government is similar in many ways and in the particular case I shall describe, they follow the same practice. If the office of viceroy or prime minister of a kingdom falls empty, the kings have two secretaries, who are those who seek advice from people of quality and talent in order to fill these positions and having consulted them, the king considers to whom he should give the post. He then orders him to come before him and tells him, by means of one of the secretaries:

"I have chosen your person for such and such a post; these are the laws and ordinances that you must keep. Read them all to him and when they have been read, tell him to look and see whether he has any problem with these laws, for breaking any of them subsequently will cost him his life. His predecessor so-and-so had a salary of so much; let him see whether he can maintain himself with that. If there is some valid reason to increase it, or if he has a larger family to support, His Majesty will easily do it, so that the lowness of the salary cannot serve as an excuse for engaging in any kind of trade or receiving gifts or bribes from anyone, for this is something that has to be punished with the greatest severity and speed. Having carried out this procedure, the new governor asks for an appropriate salary and from the day that he takes up his position, the King has secret inspectors who report on his behaviour and his truthfulness. And if in this transparency and foresight they are not barbarians, yet they seem to be so in the mercilessness and rigour with which they carry out their punishments, for almost all their laws carry the death penalty. Consequently, people are condemned to death without human intervention ever impeding its execution. As proof of which, I will tell of a case which happened to me at Usuki in the year that I was cast away.

One of the sailors who was on my boat was robbed of 8 reales by a Japanese and without thinking what he was doing, he went to complain to the magistrate of the street, for each one has its headman. They heard him, verified the theft and, having proved it, in little more than 3 hours, condemned the Japanese to death. They came in haste to tell me of it and that they already wanted to take him out to execute him. I went to the house of the magistrate who, like everyone in that land, now treated me with respect, knowing the honour and favours that the Emperor had bestowed on me. I found him in his tribunal passing judgement, in greater state than judges have with us. He recognized me from a distance and sent a message to tell me that it was not a suitable place to talk and he would come to see what I would bid him do. I waited a little while, after which he appeared with a numerous suite. He asked me to go with him to his quarters and after sitting down with me, he asked me what I wished and what I wanted him to do. I told him the matter in brief and he began to wring his hands and indicated that he was very distressed because the first thing that I asked him was impossible to grant. He told me though an interpreter to consider just how rigorous were the laws and ordinances: if the elder son of the Emperor were to come and ask what I had asked, he could not obey him, because it was the law of the kingdom that a thief who stole the value of 5 reales should die for it and the death penalty should likewise be invoked against any judge who did not carry out the sentence. And so there was no possible appeal or entreaty. I could enquire regarding the truth of this throughout the town and I would know that he could not be blamed. I told him that the plaintiff forgave the theft and brought the man who had betrayed the sailor with me, but there was nothing to be done to stop him taking him out and executing him within the hour.

But it was a fortunate loss since it led to a great gain for as the condemned man was going through the streets, he called out to

Father Francisco de Mendoza, who wore the habit of the Order of St Francis, who was with me. He took hold of him and made him go to the place where the sentence was to be carried out and there he said that for many years he had been a Christian in his heart and he wanted to die under that law. He catechized him with all the haste the situation demanded and it was done so well and with such speed that they had only just poured the water of baptism on him when the executioner arrived and cut off his head, as well as that of another who was sentenced with him for some other crime. That afternoon, the friars took me to see the two heads set up on two poles: that of our Christian had his eyes turned to heaven with the greatest devotion, while that of his companion was very different, looking down at the earth. We gave great thanks to God for His works.

With this, I close the description extolling the way in which the laws and ordinances of the King are obeyed in these kingdoms, where I was assured that it was known that for many years that no governor or Viceroy had bought or sold, nor had taken anything over and above his salary. It should fill us with shame that a godless people should show us how to keep such precepts. And although it looks as if I had set my foot in the stirrup to speak of more things relating to Japan, I will leave it for later, so as not to deprive this work of the important matter which I have begun concerning the government of Spain.

Ch XXXIV

On the Discovery of the Philippines – their Importance and Problems

Having begun to speak of the Philippines, I do not wish to pass in silence over one of the most important aspects of the monarchy, since having been given the opportunity, it would be most culpable to omit the remedies for its problems.

In the more than 60 years since these islands were discovered, they have been maintained through the Royal Exchequer[1], because there are few villages belonging to the Crown [of Your Majesty] and there are no *quintos*[2] or customs duties[3]. Furthermore, there is little hope of entering, whether by war or peace, into the vastness of China, Korea or Japan, plans which could have justified this cost, judging of course from a worldly point of view and without the divine aid through which we have seen and can see most miraculous victories.

Great China is unconquerable by force of arms because of its' size and the enormous number of its people. The experts say that in the whole of Italy there are nine million people, in Germany nineteen and in the *Paises* [sic] five, in France fifteen, in Spain seven, in Sicily one and a half, in England three and the Low Countries three, which add up to sixty two, while China has seventy[4] The assessment of the income is one hundred and thirty million in gold escudos, which is not very much for 600 very large cities, 1,500 towns and 1,100 fortified castles, not to mention innumerable villages, as well as the cities of Nunquit[5] and Panguina[6], which take a whole day to cross.

Japan too is unconquerable and the example of Hernando Cortes is remote and nonsensical, because New Spain was a very small matter compared to these kingdoms and a Japanese is worth a hundred Indians in terms of courage and spirit. This slams the door on any idea that some ill-informed person might have of attempting a similar undertaking, placing all their reliance on the valour of the Spaniards and underestimating the very unequal opposing force.

By peaceful means, such as the preaching of the Holy Gospel, through the infinite power of God and the finite means of human men, it is possible that great triumphs and victories can be achieved and won along this path. However, the hardness and obstinacy of these people opposes us, if the blood shed by so many martyrs does not soften their hearts. And even should God wish to open the gates in this way, the kings would remain as they are and the kingdoms in their power and Spain would have no other share than the glory of having spread the Faith – which is no small matter – and the friendship of such powerful kings. They are so because of the great number and wealth of their subjects, proving that the contrary in our Spain is what weakens and undermines her. The following is a matter of state to which much attention is paid in China and Japan: that the kings should be content with what they have and seek to conserve it without being distracted, or bleeding themselves [i.e. the State] with expeditions and new conquests. Thus it was in Japan that the Emperor Taikosama was persuaded by some of his captains to put 80,000 men into the field – and to give an idea of his power, levied and trained them in twenty days, after which he sent them to conquer Korea, a very powerful kingdom next to China, which is no more than six leagues[7] crossing away. He conquered it in only three days, installed a viceroy there and enjoyed possession of it, without being challenged by anyone. However, after a year, seeing that it was very far, although there is an island of Japan sixty leagues from Korea, he dismantled it all and left it to its inhabitants, considering it an embarrassment and of no use to his crown.

Would that it might please our Lord God that Your Majesty should promulgate an inviolable law decreeing that all new conquests should cease and so no longer drain away the strength of Spain on their account, thus weakening her through the need to maintain what has already been won, which is very great and which Your Majesty can barely encompass with your royal arms, long as they are. And, my lord, an excess of the unnecessary leads to a lack of the essential.

Let Your Majesty consider how many people live in China[8], in New Mexico, Sinaloa[9], and other parts of New Spain and Peru, and you will see how all these people left Spain, which greatly misses them, both for herself and for her naval wars. Above all, in the Philippines more than 50,000 men have died in the past fifty years and have taken there more than forty million [? reales] from New Spain. Sire, what king less powerful than you would not be impoverished by the loss of forty millions and 30,000 [sic] men? And this silver enriches the Chinese and the Japanese, and never returns to Spain except in the form of some plates and bowls and wretched silks, which do no more than attract at first sight, so that both poor and rich are cheated into buying them. However, I would not have set down a description of these ills, if it were not to find a remedy for them. Someone who has looked into these matters could reply that this has already been done, since the Council[10], by means of many orders and edicts has decreed that no money should pass to the Philippines. If this were carried out as it should be, there would be nothing wrong, but the world is such that there is always someone who profits, even in the execution of a royal command.

The Viceroy sends someone who seems suitable to the port of Acapulco, but what seems suitable to this man is to take a cut of 10-12% in order to allow the silver to be shipped. The news spreads and the merchants trading there consider this bribe very cheap. In China, the mother who bears a son who does not trade and traffic holds herself unlucky. The agent here claims that it took place outside the kingdom. Some lend to him, others do him service; they all live off China and Your Majesty dies of it. The governor of China [i.e. the Philippines] plays deaf and blind so that the same thing can take place here. Your Majesty is far distant and although respect for Your Majesty should always be close at hand, everything is destroyed, bankrupted by untrustworthy ministers who are blinded and dragged (this way and that) by greed. Your Majesty, contrive to choose them with care and punish those who transgress and reward the faithful ones. I think it would be best to close the port of Acapulco[11] and aid for the Philippines should go from Cadiz or Lisbon, leaving there at the safe season and returning to the same port with the merchandise from China. As to the journey to New Spain, the soldiers land at Veracruz and go on from there to Mexico and Acapulco, but the differences in climate and the bad roads kill half of them, while others flee, which in no way produces the desired result.

Notes

1.   *Hacienda*
2.   *Quinto del* Rey, goes back to the Muslim occupation of the Iberian peninsula – mentioned for example in the legal code of Yusuf I of Granada (1318-1354) – and gave the ruler 20% of any treasure discovered or spoils of war.
3.   *Almojarifazgo* – a tax dating back to the 14th century – customs dues levied on goods entering or leaving Spanish territory, or as here passing between Spanish ports in the Spanish colonies, for example Manila and Acapulco.
4.   JM suggests that Vivero may have got his population statistics from Giovanni Botero, whose *Relazioni* were translated into Spanish as *Descripción de todas las provincias del mundo,* Barcelona, 1622.
5.   Perhaps Nanjing
6.   Probably Beijing [Pekin]
7.   The nautical league in the Hispanic world at this date was usually calculated as roughly 6km (3.73 miles). The Korea Strait is actually c.200km (120 miles). For a more realistic account of these wars, see the Introduction.
8.   This was the period of the Iberian Union, so the term would refer to Macao, Formosa (Taiwan), etc., as well as the Philippines and other Spanish colonies in the East.
9.   State in north-western Mexico.
10.   *Consejo de Indias* or Council of the Indes was the principal body controlling the administration of the Spanish Empire in America and Asia; its archives are now lodged in the Archivo General de Indias in Seville. Trade policies were set by the Casa de la Contratación, also in Seville.
11.   This had already been suggested in 1612 (see JM n.192) and, earlier still, Pedro Bravo de Acuña, who governed the Philippines from 1602-6, suggested that the Spanish should establish a stopping point at Monterey on the California coast, which would have the added advantage that returning ships could by-pass Japan.

Ch XLIV

On the refinement of its places and kingdoms and the splendid possessions] held by that king.

In 1609, I left the position of Governor and Captain General[1] of the Philippines, my successor in these offices and in that of President of the *Audiencia*[2] was Don Juan de Silva[3], who was born in Jerez, but raised trained in Flanders, where he had been a cavalry officer. This background is not the most appropriate to fill a post of such importance, where quite other qualities are needed.

He arrived in March at the port of Cavite and as I had ready the galleon, the *San Francisco*, as well as two others, and as I was leaving the government, it was he who was to start the lading of them. He began this matter, and the other tasks that fell to him, so blindly and so incompetently that in more than 40 days he had still not completed the official paperwork, nor had prepared the vitally important clearance document[4] although completing it in time determines success or failure.

Wanting to name one of his relatives or household as General[5] and thinking that he could contrive to do it, he offered the post to Don Juan Ronquillo[6] an officer of the court[7], a man who aspired to higher things and whom it was obvious should not be chosen, and the same applied to a certain Don Juan Esquerra, a very old man and already retired, who could be similarly judged.

Don Juan replied that he could not go, but Juan Esquerra immediately accepted, ambition being still so strong in an old man of 70 with neither the strength nor the spirit for such a position. With this man as General, things proceeded very slowly, so that we did not sail from the port of Cavite until the 15th of July. I was on board the galleon, the *San Francisco*, which left the mouth of the river most successfully, but in the neighbourhood of the Ladrones[8], on the 10th August, tempests began that were so numerous and violent that up until the 30th, on which date this galleon was wrecked, we never had four days without hurricanes and the wildest weather that ever has been known at sea. The galleon was strong and more than 1,000 tons, but badly constructed, so that sometimes we had 30 men at the helm and yet that was not sufficient. We were running close under Japan, but as the cockpit was under fourteen hands[9]of water, we decided to cut down the main mast and make for shore. But with five pilots on board, a mistake of more than a degree was made in calculating the elevation and a mistake of more than two on the sea chart, so that we were heading round the furthest point of Japan when, at 10 o'clock at night, we struck the coast and the village of Yubanda, where for two leagues there are rocks on which the ship was immediately broken to pieces and 56 people drowned. The rest of us saved ourselves by means of planks, or as best we could. God allowed a section of the poop to remain by which means most escaped at dawn, for in the dark night we could all have perished there. The richest barely escaped with his shirt and I lost a large chest that I was bringing with me. It was made in China and, with some rubies and diamonds, all together were worth more than 100,000 ducats, but I remained grateful to God that He left the greatest riches of all: my life.

The vessel, the *Santa Ana*, which left at the same time as us, arrived at the port of Usique[10] and the *Santiago* reached New Spain. We came out of it with nothing and we did not know where we were. At first we thought we were on some uninhabited island until we saw a horde of Japanese, who asked who was the *acha*[11], that is to say the chief or captain. On saying that it was myself, they led me, bound like all the others, to the village by a very bad road. There they made us captives and prisoners and would not let us leave until they had told the *tono*, who is their lord, and he had informed the Emperor. They told this *tono* – who is something like a grandee in Spain – that I was the Governor of the Philippines and he came to see me and brought two of the robes that they wear, which are something like the robes worn by judges and some gifts of food, including a cow, the flesh of which it is a great crime to eat according to their law. He asked me to go by way of his house, if the Emperor summoned me to his court, and this I did. He has a very strong castle with a moat and a very cleverly designed drawbridge.

Having spent 48 days, an English pilot[12] came, married there more than 20 years, whom the Emperor favours. He brought me a safe conduct to leave this prison and a *chapa*, which is a royal permit, to go to the city of Surunga, the Emperor's court, without anyone interfering with me or offering me insults, or demanding money for food and the necessities of travel. He [Vivero's "Emperor" – in fact, the Shogun] sent to tell me that regarding all the things that had washed up on the beach, although according to the laws of the kingdom they were his, yet he made me a gift of them. There was no lack of lawyers who were of the opinion that I could take them, but I did not do so – on the contrary, I had them handed over to the captain of the galleon, saying that he should return them to their owners in Manila, for I did not wish to enrich myself with the possessions of so many poor people.

This done, I went, very well looked-after, to the city of Yendo [Edo – modern Tokyo], 40 leagues before one reaches the court, where the eldest son of the emperor lives and holds his own court. I asked permission to see it and it was granted me. This palace of the prince and his authority are no less great than that of his father whom he succeeded, to the great prejudice of Christianity in Japan, for he is its mortal enemy. He gave me six of his robes, two splendid swords they call *katanas*[13] and two sets of armour, richer than ours, but not so strong.

After this I went on to Surunga where the Emperor was. Yendo where the prince lives is a better place for it has 150,000 inhabitants, while Surunga has 100,000 and the palace is also better and more luxurious than the one at Yendo. Having reached the court at Surunga, on the following day the Emperor sent his secretary to visit me at the house of a gentleman with whom, on his orders, I was being lodged and he sent me twelve very fine robes of his and four swords with a tactful message telling me that I was most welcome and that for one who had escape naked, the best present that one could offer would be a gift of clothes, and that I should wear them, even though they were different from our dress. He bade me rest and all that was needful for myself and for my comfort, he would give me in abundance. The secretary remained with me asking various questions and my host and other Japanese gentlemen warned me not to ask to see the Emperor until an order came from him bidding me to go.

I remained in this limbo eight days, enjoying a very beautiful house and admiring the grandeur of those places, at the end of which one morning the same secretary of the Emperor returned to see me and, as he was taking his leave, said:

"When would you like to see the Emperor?"

I said that whenever His Highness gave me permission, I would take it as a very great favour. He replied:

"Then you could go this afternoon and I will send you the palace guard to escort you and one of the Emperor's litters in which you can ride."

These are carried like our sedan chairs. I thanked him and they notified me that at two in the afternoon the guard, composed of more than 200 arquebusiers, was coming, as well as the sedan chair, which I got into. After travelling a considerable distance, we arrived at a moat with a drawbridge, which was immediately raised from the castle, until signals were given by the guard that it should be lowered. Then, a captain came out to greet me, preceded by 30 halberdiers, and he called at a very strongly fortified iron door, which they opened and there were two 200 arquebusiers, all armed. The captain took me through the midst of them, a matter of 500 paces, to another moat, also with a drawbridge. There he left me in the charge of another captain and on opening the door to me, I found 200 halberdiers lined up, all armed, with some arquebusiers among them. I was led forward with the greatest show of courtesy until I came into a corridor of the palace and in the first chamber I entered, I saw more than 1,000 men, arquebusiers on one side and halberdiers on the other.

In each chamber and separate area, I was received by gentlemen of the palace, until I had passed through eight or nine apartments. There was so much to admire in their construction – the ceilings were ablaze with gold and the walls had a thousand paintings, like those on the screens that they send here, but of better quality. Two rooms before the one where the Emperor was, two of his secretaries came out to receive me and invited me to rest for a while, which I duly did. Consecundono[14] , who was the elder of them, spoke to me in the following terms – that it seemed opportune to tell me of the greatness of the Emperor of Japan, who was the greatest monarch in all the world and his kingdoms and his vassals respected him as such. This, to the extent that when a *tono* – who is like one of our grandees and some have incomes of two million – comes to see the Emperor and is within a hundred paces of his throne, he kneels and bows his head to the ground without raising it to the Emperor and this without the latter saying a word to show satisfaction or gratitude at receiving the present that has been brought, he returns to his house and estates. Since this was the long-established custom and royal ceremonies could not be abrogated, the Emperor was concerned that I should not mistake the attitude he was forced to take with me for dryness and had wished that I should be warned of it.

To this I replied by the mouth of Father Juan Buaptista [sic] and another Father of the Company that I had listened most attentively to his very well presented reasons and rejoiced to know of the greatness of the Emperor, which could not dismay me, because I was the vassal of the King Don Felipe, my lord, who was even more so, being a giant among the kings of this world, while the others compared to him were but dwarfs. I went on to tell him a number of specific things, extending myself on the subject as much as I could. I agreed that kings had to act strictly towards their vassals and not break with the ceremonies of royalty, but with those who were not their subjects, they should, for excellent reasons of state show themselves as straightforward and agreeable.

I said that I had been sent by my king to govern the Philippine Islands, where I held the posts of Captain General and President, and that returning to Spain had run into tempests and contrary winds and thus was wrecked off Japan, where, I pointed out, I was initially treated not only as a vassal, but as a captive and if the Emperor chose to treat me thus, measuring his civilities to my mischance and ill fortune, any small favour would seem a great one to me. But if he decided to have me treated as a servant of my King and as his representative, coming in his name, the honour should be greater and if it were not, that would concern my King and not me; but having told him this, he should do as he thought fit.

The secretary struck his forehead with his hand and told me that he wished to go back and speak to the Emperor. Within a quarter of an hour he came out again and said that I should go in and that I should be very glad for the Emperor was doing me an honour never before seen in Japan.

I went in and found myself in a great chamber, divided in two by three steps at the top of which were two grills, which in Spain we would assume to be gilt, but there were most certainly gold and proceeded to where the Emperor was sitting on a round throne covered in green velvet. He wore a flowing robe of something like gold tabby and green silk with two *katanas* at his waist and his hair all plaited. He was a venerable old man, stout, and more than 70 years old. I stopped six or eight paces from his seat, having been warned not to approach to kiss his hand – from fear and prudence these kings do not wish anyone to approach them.

Having reached this point, after the customary courtesies, I remained standing. He gestured to me twice; that I should sit and that I should cover my head, and he remained looking at me for a moment, then clapped his hands twice at which a gentleman, no doubt of his chamber, came forward from where he had remained prostrated with ten or twelve others behind the grill. He sent him to call one of the two secretaries who were with me and told him to tell me that the Emperor was happy to see me and that my travails should not make me melancholy, for the spirit of a gentleman should not be cast down by a misfortune at sea and that I should ask for favours and he would grant them as generously as my own king. I rose to answer him, but he bade me sit down again and I said that although in truth my losses and troubles could very reasonably make me melancholy, yet the presence of kings had the power to alleviate the worst misfortunes and thus the favour that His Highness had shown me was already making it possible for the past to be forgotten and I would not be slow to ask favours of so great a king that he would grant in the course of time. He replied that I should proceed to say what I wanted and the secretary insisted that I should not delay, and so I told him the three things that I had to ask of His Highness.

The first was that the Friars and the Fathers of the Company in those kingdoms should not be maltreated, but rather be allowed to preach the Holy Gospel freely and with as much safety as do the many *bonsos*[16] of different sects.

Secondly, I entreated him not to allow certain Dutch pirate corsairs who were in one of his ports, because they were enemies of my king and it was not fitting for one so great as His Highness to protect and favour thieves.

The third thing that I asked was that in virtue of the enduring peace and friendship with Your Majesty, he should give orders that Manila ships that came here or were forced to take shelter should be given a good welcome.

He listened to everything very carefully and said that he would reply, and although I wanted to rise and take my leave, he bade me stay. At this point a *tono*, a great lord, came in from outside and kneeling at the door of the chamber, he almost kissed the ground. He had before him a table and set on it were a number of gold bars that I was told would be worth 100,000 ducats. He ordered that I should be shown the palace.

Two days later, the secretary Consecundono brought me his reply. It said that the Friars and Priests would be allowed in his kingdoms and that no one should persecute them. As to the Dutch, he did not know whether they were thieves or corsairs, but that they had his word that for two years he would leave them in the port where they were, but when that time was up he assured me that he would turn them out of his kingdoms and that it pleased him very well to preserve the friendship of so great a king as Your Majesty. Also, that he would show great favour and generosity to any of your subjects who might be driven ashore or otherwise find themselves in Japan, and that if I should need anything for myself, I should tell him.

I spent eleven months at this court and in Miyako [Kyoto] and at the end of which he gave me a ship with which to return and 4,000 ducats to equip it. He then sent the Father, Brother Alonso Muñoz, with some Japanese and a present for Your Majesty. On the return from Mexico, he was brought a certain number of things that he had asked me for, such as black silk serge[17], red wine, clocks and other trifles that did not add up to much. It is certain that if this Emperor had lived, Christian affairs would have increased and prospered.

He died within two years and although kingdoms are not passed on by inheritance, the prince his son had thoroughly won the general good will, with the result that they raised him to the throne of that great monarchy which is Japan. It is divided into 76 provinces that they call kingdoms[18].

There are three large islands and other small ones adjacent. They call one of these islands Ximo[19], which means the low kingdoms, as opposed to Miyako and the Court, and Kyushu[20], which means nine kingdoms, because that is the number of them on that island. It is the most westerly and is where the ships of China and Manila normally arrive. It runs north-south and is very broad and has many bays and inlets of the sea both south and west.

The second is called Shikoku[21] which means "four kingdoms" and some call it Tensa because one of its kingdoms is called Tosa[22]. It is separated from the first by an arm of the sea that lies between them running east-west.

The third island is the largest[23]. It begins from the tip of the first, to the north and east, and runs in an easterly direction above the second. Then it turns west and to the south there is a cape, which the Spaniards call the Devil's Cape, in the kingdom of Kinokuni[24] There are two other capes, one to the north at the mid-point of Japan and another at the far end on the coast opposite Yendo [Edo – modern Tokyo]. From the headland on which the galleon, the *San Francisco*, was lost in the year 1609 on the 30th September, to Yubanda is a league and a half. So, the kingdom at the lowest latitude is that of Satsuma in Kyushu[25], which lies at 31 ½ ° and the highest is on the coast opposite Edo, which although our pilots have it at 34°, in fact runs to 41° and beyond. The great city of Miyako stands at 35° and Surunga and Yendo, which are the courts in the east of Japan, are almost at the same latitude.

This is land is composed of 50 kingdoms and around it there are many islands, all inhabited, with large numbers of people. Three have the title of kingdom – the two to the north are densely populated and have many silver mines, the other is to the south. West of these lies Great China and with a moderate wind one can make the journey in three or four days. Between China and Japan there is a peninsula running from 34° up to 40°, at which point it is contiguous to China and so close that only an arm of the sea an arquebus shot wide, forming an inlet, separates them.

To the north, there is the kingdom of Urangai, which is *terra firma*, part of the same landmass as Korea and Tartary. North-east of Miyako and north of the northernmost point of Japan is Yeso[26], with which the Japanese have trade relations, but it is unclear whether it is an island or *terra firma* and merges into Urangai. To the south, as far as is known, there are no islands or lands of any importance, but to the south west there is the Ysla Hermosa[27][Taiwan] and below that the Philippine Islands.

Speaking of the origins of this land, they say that in ancient times there were some rustic inhabitants and that their kings took their origins from some *kami*[28] of heaven or earth – an ancient custom of many illustrious people who claim descent from the gods. What is known, however, from tradition and reliable histories, is that their kings are descended from a king of China and that the first king of Japan was called Ginmatenno[29], who began his reign 663 years before Christ, our Lord, and 89 years after the founding of Rome. And, as is the case with no other nation in the world, it then remained in the same family and in a direct line 108 generations, some 2260 years. Until roughly 60 years ago, they had no dealings with any other country, except China and their books and learning and religion came from there, and the ceremonies surrounding the kings of Japan are very similar and carry the same symbolism as those of the king of China.

In the past, those known as *dairios*[30]and their families ruled, and soldiers were not as highly regarded then as they are in Japan today. More than 450 years ago, two of these families of warriors[31], descended from the *dairios*, rebelled and as first one prevailed and then the other, all that remained to the kings was their name. They had to distribute honours and rewards with the very small income that they had, but which also had to suffice for the maintenance of their household and palace. These kings were called Daire or Teivo[32] and they always live in the great city of Miyako, which has more than 800,000 inhabitants. They do not leave the city, nor can they ever set foot to ground, nor can they ever be seen by anyone, except those of a certain rank, and by their women.

The Emperors [i.e. shoguns]] are called *Toncadoni*[33]and their position is secure. They are also called *Cubozama*, which is the same – *sama* means lord and *cubo* means something like Capitán General or dictator, as the Romans called him. This position of emperor is conferred by the Daire and he goes to receive it before beginning to govern[34].

Japan has never been conquered nor dominated by any other nation, although the Chinese and Koreans have sometimes come seeking a fight, but they have always gone back with their hands on their heads[35].

As I said earlier, they are men of very lively wit and extremely courteous to each other. The left side, which we give to inferiors, is their right and they do much honour to whoever it is offered, because they show great trust placing him next to their sword. They are very fine arquebusiers, although they draw very slowly. They are skilled with the lance but, although they have had artillery in these parts for 60 years, they are not expert with it. The great lords have castles impossible to take by siege and all make use of the ruses and strategies of war.

The political government of their towns is excellent and those who govern pay extraordinary attention to public matters. The houses are extremely well-kept and remarkably clean, and this applies even to the streets. The country is very rich in gold and silver, and if there were mining technicians and quicksilver, they would get a greater yield.

Rice is the normal food, although their wheat is better than that in Spain and gives a high yield, since one *fanega*[36] produces 50. They eat bread as dessert, and very little of it and they do not eat any meat, except what they kill hunting, but they have more game and fish than us. Deer, rabbits, partridges, grebes or wild duck[37] and all sorts of game birds cover the countryside and the lagoons.

The kingdom of Boju[38] is very rich in gold and on its headland they pick cotton from which they make blankets, and they also produce hemp. The nobles wear silk but Japanese silk is not good, so they bring it each year from China, with much painting and needlework. The nobles go with a great train of followers and the workmen and ordinary people so respect them that they prostrate themselves on the ground when they pass along the street.

The varnish on their writing tables and desks is like a resin obtained from a tree and there is nothing to equal it, and so they have the most strange and enchanting objects of this kind.

Their swords and *katanas* are also most remarkable, for there are *katanas* valued at 100,000 ducats and it is absolutely established that they can cut a man sitting with his legs crossed from top to bottom. They laugh at us because we place a high value on a diamond or a ruby, saying that only swords are beyond price.

The nobles of Japan are like our titled aristocracy and with *mero mixto*[39] have dominion over everything on their estates and they give or withhold income from them to their household and families as they chose. If they are deprived of their estates or move from them, all their people move with them. Their vassals are obliged to offer their services in both war and peace and are regularly required to provide their lord with an escort and thus he is well-served and greatly respected. And they apply to them in temporal matters.

In their idolatry, they worship the *kamis*, who were those of their forefathers in some way notable and they turn to them in temporal matters, but they ask the *fotogues*[40], who were men from the Kingdom of Siam and Pegu for their salvation. They have great temples with learned priests who preach and hold solemn ceremonies, as well as funerals and services for the dead.

The temple of Taikosama[41] in the city of Miyako and his tomb is one of the most impressive; it could even be considered one of the Seven Marvels. There, they raised a metal statue, which, with the temple in which it stands, they say cost 24 million and that 100,000 people worked on it. I went to see it and asked permission to climb the steps up to the top. Thinking I should bring something back to give an idea of its size, I sent one of my servants, who was a very willing lad, to take the measurements of this Daibu, as they call this idol. He laughed at me and said that he could not even manage the fingers. At last he succeeded in measuring the thumb of his right hand by putting his arm round it, but even so, two handbreadths were lacking to encircle it completely.

I went in to the main part of their accursed church, where they have stoups with accursed water, just as we have holy water . Before uncovering the ashes of the Taiko, they prostrate themselves on the ground and remove six veils of different brocades until a grill appears and there they are in an urn of gold. They worship them with great cries and then cover them again. Truly, that day I noted the devotion shown by the women and men in their temple: they were not distracted by talking, and even kept the custody of their eyes and maintained a noteworthy silence. We should feel great shame that we, who have the true faith, are so different in our lack of devotion and total absence of respect.

Notes

1 *Capitán-General* – Admiral of the Fleet.
2 Essentially Court of Appeals. The *Audiencia Real* (usually *Real Audiencia)* were high tribunals to which all of criminal and civil sentences in a given territory could be sent for appeal.
3 De Silva was in fact from Trujillo. He spent much of his time on campaign and gained a great reputation for courage in his fights against the Dutch, although he was unsuccessful in stopping their advances into the Iberian sphere of influence. In poor health, he asked repeatedly to be relieved of his command and died at Malacca in 1616. Documents relating to his time in office can be

found in *The Philippine Islands, 1493-1898: Volume XVII, 1606-16* ed. Emma Helen Blair and James Alexander Robertson, on-line at www.gutenberg.org/ebooks/15530. Vivero was, of course, irritated at a) not having been confirmed as Governor and b) having to leave too late in the season.

4   *Memoria de despacho*

5   Perhaps Capitán General de la Armada – the person in charge of the defense of the convoy of ships in the *Carrera de Indias*.

6   Ronquillo had been in charge of the unsuccessful campaign against Mindanao at the very end of the 16th century under the governorship of Francisco de Tello de Guzmán.

7   *Alguacil*

8   From the late 18th c. known as the Marianas.

9   *Palmo* – a very variable unit of measurement, anywhere between 3"/8cm and 9"/23cm. In this case, something approaching the former makes more sense.

10   In Kyushu

11   The Japanese word has not been identified.

12   Will Adams

13   *Cathana* – single edged sword, particularly those used by the samurai.

14   Presumably Kōzuke no suke – title of the chief secretary

15   *Tabi* – a striped or, by this date, watered silk taking its name from the al-'Attābiyya district of Baghdad

16   From the Japanese *bonzo* – a Buddhist priest, hence obsolete English bonze.

17   *Rajas* – at this date almost certainly the very valuable silk twill – it is mentioned as highly desirable in Don Quixote.

18   The confusion comes from the Japanese word *kuni* (country) also being used for provinces. The provinces were established in the 7th century and continued until the beginning of the Meiji era, 1868, but the exact count varied. Vivero elsewhere gives 50 and 66, the latter being more correct at that date.

19   From *shima* – island.

20   Quiusit

21   Xicocu

22   The old name for the province now Kochi Prefecture.

23   Hondo, modern Honshu.

24   Quinocun – Kii Peninsula

25   Jacuma. South-western Kyushu, part of modern Kagoshima Province.

26   Modern Ezo. The term refers to the lands to the north of Japan and can mean Hokkaido, Sakhalin, the Kuril Islands, etc.

27   Formosa, i.e. the Beautiful Island.

28   *Camiselestes*, from *kami* – spirits, natural forces, deities + the Spanish *celeste* – heavenly

29   Jinmu-tenno – "God Warrior Emperor" – the first emperor of Japan and descendant of Amaterasu-omikami the sun goddess. His date of birth is generally given as 711 B.C.; there is much debate as to what extent he is purely legendary.

30   *Daimyo*

31   The Taira and the Minamoto clans, and the Genpei War – the civil war – of 1180-85, leading to the establishment of the Kamakura Shogunate in 1192.

32   Perhaps *Taiko* – title given to a retired Kampaku or regent

33   Perhaps *takadono* – Lord of the universe.

34   See *Introduction* for the general misunderstanding concerning Emperor and Shogun.

35   Probably referring to the Mongol invasions of 1274 and 1281, launched by Kublai Khan, founder of the Yuan Dynasty, from Beijing via Korea.

36   A measure of dry capacity, often given as 55.5 litres.

37   *Lavanco*. As Buddhists, the Japanese were squeamish about meat, but several of the most hunted animals were renamed to make eating them seem more licit. Wild boar became *yamakujira* – mountain whale – while hares were reclassified as birds, perhaps because of their large wing-like ears.

38   Boshu on the Chiba Peninsula.

39   Medieval legal term: *mero et mixto imperio* – the absolute powers and rights granted to a feudal lord.

40   *Hotoke* – the Buddha, a statue of the Buddha, a bodhisattva or someone who has attained enlightenment.

41   The title frequently used in the Catholic sources for Toyotomi Hideyoshi (c. 1536-1598), Taiko being a retired *kampaku* – chief advisor or regent. This account of the Daibutsu, or Great Buddha, is somewhat confusing. In 1588, Hideyoshi banned peasants from owning weapons (and samurai from working on the land, thus hardening the lines between classes) and all the confiscated swords were melted down and used to form a Daibutsu, intended to surpass the famous one at Nara, at a temple founded by Hideyoshi – Hoko-ji. In 1596, both Daibutsu and temple were destroyed in an earthquake. Work was begun to replace them, but they were again destroyed when fire broke out in 1602. In 1610, Hideyoshi's son Toyotomi Hideyori, decided to rebuild the temple, following his father's plans, create a new Daibutsu and cast the largest bell in Japan, the inscription on which was later to have disastrous political repercussions for the clan. This sequence of events makes it hard to understand exactly what Vivero could have seen, although his description is plausible. The Daibutsu at Nara is officially given the following measurements:
Height: 14.98 m (49.1 ft)
Face: 5.33 m (17.5 ft)
Eyes: 1.02 m (3.3 ft)
Nose: 0.5 m (1.6 ft)
Ears: 2.54 m (8.3 ft)
The statue weighs c.500 tons

Ch XLV

Continuing on the subject of the Japanese, their marriages and the way that they treat their women and that they do not have the custom of dowries – a practice that would not be at all bad for Spain

The political government of Japan is the best that I know of in all the states of the world and it is shaming that a godless people should have such perfect laws and so in tune with charity. In this country, vice is punished as I mentioned earlier with the result that there are few thieves and the roads are extremely safe. Vagabonds are not allowed, since there are judges who deal with them and set them to work in their towns and villages, according to whatever aptitude they have and the occupations of their fathers. There are authorities in charge of tilling and ploughing, so that rice, barley and wheat are sown in great quantity and the peasants enjoy many privileges and favours.[1]

They do not keep cattle in the fields yet, even without that, it is still the land with the most large livestock of any known, for the poorest man owns two cows or oxen, and the rich many more. These animals eat hay and barley in stables like horses and are so docile that they have them carry loads. They make something like a very high pack saddle or pannier and a Japanese sits on the load of wheat, rice or barley controlling the ox or cow or even bull with a rope in its mouth. They go along at the speed of a horse and stop at the doors and sell what they are carrying, then they return to their stables and mangers, so that they can be described as domesticated, like those that we breed up for home use on our estates.

There are also authorities in charge of boats and sailors, who have wood cut and ropes, anchors and other necessary material prepared, and no-one leaves port without having been checked to see that they are taking suitable equipment and crew.

As to what they call spirituality and religion, one must admire the care with which the priests look after the temples in their charge and the exquisite attention paid to the materials for their construction, as well as the punctuality of their hours of prayer to the devil, whereby they waste their time and do great damage to themselves.

There are no fights over women, because the public prostitutes are established by legal decree, which sets what is to be given to them, and there is a doctor who examines them and, if they have some infectious disease, isolates them with remarkable rigour. Those who so wish, come and go to their houses and no questions are ever asked. Even if they are very ordinary women and wives of artisans, it is extremely rare to hear of a married woman who has done her husband wrong. They all marry without dowries and although the lords and gentlemen have as many as they consider befits their status – for this is how it is judged – and some have more than fifty or sixty, the first is considered the most important lady and her children are the most favoured; nevertheless, she is not to take offence at seeing favours bestowed on any of the others. The very poor have only one wife and others two or four, depending on their means. The wives of the nobility see neither the sun nor the moon, brothers nor parents, and rarely even their children. They go out to the temple in closed litters called *orimones*[2] and with a large headdress which falls to the breast, so that no-one can, by any chance, see them.

A gentleman seeks to know the qualities of a maiden – her claims to nobility, her chastity, her sweetness of temper, her character and her beauty and this is all the dowry he seeks before asking her parents for her. They give nothing with her[3], because it would be considered an affront to the suitor – for it is he who makes gifts to the father and other relatives. And since they neither ask nor give thousands as dowries, they preserve a greater prosperity in the houses of both rich and poor. Would that Spain would follow this example as a policy of state. For some rob the whole world in order to provide their daughter with a dowry and these days her other qualities are not considered before seeking her out. The only question is: how great is her dowry?

Your Majesty should order an enquiry into the pros and cons of this matter and so much would be discovered regarding this matter that it would come close to being one of the most important subjects in Spain. If dowries could be abolished or moderated, it would do much to alleviate the country's poverty. And, pushing this line of thought further, it would lead to an increase in virtue, given that choice would be made on that ground alone. Women who did not come to their marriages with dowries would not be in a position to be arrogant towards their husbands. Aristotle reproached the Lacadaemonians for allowing great dowries to be given, considering it better that they should marry without, or at least that they should be moderate. *Intoleravilius nihil est quam femina dives* – nothing is as intolerable as a wealthy woman – and it is clear that the husband who receives a large dowry is forced because of that to show a measure of respect not fitting to the superiority of a husband. He cannot deny her the finery, ornaments and jewels that she says are owing to her for what she brought. And no lesser person than St Peter himself said that the lack of obedience to their husbands on the part of married women is born of the frivolity of their adornments and worldly dress. Ending the custom of giving them dowries would teach them humility. This can be deduced from the example of Sara who obeyed Abraham and called him her lord and St Ambrose says that it was because he married her without a dowry, for those that have large ones will not humble themselves, something which is most amply proved[4].

It would be extremely useful to put a stop to the complicated proceeding with which illustrious houses – and indeed all – seek to procure dowries for their daughters, who are in general more numerous than the sons, and the imbalance in the dowries makes for an imbalance in status, because gold levels everything out. The Chanceries and Courts are overrun with cases connected with the restitution of dowries, which is no small inconvenience, nor is it a small matter to force and do violence to the wishes and inclinations of daughters, for fathers, having no great dowries to give them, make them take the veil by force and enter the convent, where they live and die unfulfilled and dissatisfied. These are the reasons which have led me to the conclusion that, although abolishing dowries would be difficult, it is most desirable that they should be curbed.

This, in short, is the custom in Japan and it is upheld by the common people and by the nobles and gentlemen and, as has

142

already been said, the respect and veneration for tradition is so strong that even if a man of humble origins becomes very rich, he does not dare attempt to ally himself with noble blood, nor oppose them in anything. This is an example which, if the Spaniards were to follow, there would not be so many blood lines stained purely on account of financial interests.

Notes

1. Here, Vivero overstates the case. The peasants never had the – theoretical – high status that they had in China, but conditions had probably improved with the end of the civil wars. In any case, it is interesting that Vivero saw them as prosperous compared to Mexico or Spain.
2. *Norimon* – a palanquin, carried by two, four or more men. It was an upper-class prerogative, described together with other aspects of travel in Japan by Engelbert Kaempfer (c.1691-2)
3. The smallness and general unimportance of dowries was much commented on by foreigners, although both they and the Japanese themselves often considered that this led to more casual divorce. See *Divorce in Japan: family, gender, and the state, 1600-2000*, Harald Fuess, Stamford U.P. 2004, p.85, etc.
4. Not, perhaps, a popular view today, but Vivero may have been speaking from the heart: a good deal of the wealth in his family entered through the female line.

Ch XLVI

On the difference in character between the Japanese and the Chinese; the Japanese priding themselves on being warlike and courageous, the Chinese on being gentle, moderate and long-suffering, and on the great restraint of the Chinese as regards the favours which the lords and great men distribute, following the example of their king.

The Japanese nation prides itself on its valour and arrogance, which is more in keeping with barbarians than with wise and reasonable people, for they are not only daring in battle, but they prefer to kill themselves rather than have the executioner do it when they are condemned to death for some crime. On such an occasion, it is perceived as an act of nobility to gather together relatives, friends and fellow gentlemen, so that this assembly can bear witness that they died with courage and without fear, and they entrust their children to them. Then, they seize the *katana*[1] that they wear girded at their waists and cut themselves across the middle with such courage or mercilessness that they remain with half their body separated [from the other] and are praised by those present, invited to this bestial and barbarous event. This nation is not at all generous in giving and is generally impatient and ill-humoured. The Chinese and the Sangleys[2] are not so brave and set great store by patience....

Notes

[1] *Cathana*

[2] *Sangley*, from the Chinese *ch'ang-lai or sang-lei,* was the name given by the Spaniards in the Philippines to the pure-blood Chinese who came there in order to trade and subsequently settled. A major revolt of the *sangley* at Manila in 1603, was suppressed with great blood-shed by one of Vivero's predecessors as governor, Luìs Pérez Dasmariñas, helped by Japanese troops.

Conclusion by Roderigo de Vivero's grandson

Having gathered together such information as I was able to find and establish through notebooks [*cuadernos*] and old papers, the originals of which had been presented to the Council, and resulted in those honours that will be seen later, I continued going through documents from which were extracted copies of private letters, including one from His Majesty, the King, our lord, which I thought good to copy first, following it with others that came to light and adding an account of particular services, so that time does not efface these memories. I am doing this not so much as an obligation, but through a wish to bring back to life one who with time has become far distant from the attention of almost all, as is fitting for the grandson and successor of the aforesaid Don Roderigo de Vivero, first Conde del Valle and Vizconde de San Miguel.

The Letter which Don Rodrigo de Vivero wrote to the King, our Master

Sire, Your Majesty ordered me to go and serve him as governor and *Capitan General*[1] of the Philippines, but Don Juan de Silva having been appointed to succeed me, I turned the post over to him in the year 1609 and on the 25th of July embarked for New Spain on the *San Francisco*.

After many storms and tempests, the ship was wrecked on the reefs off the kingdom of Japan and, by the special mercy of God, I was among those saved. For forty days, I was held in a village six days distant from the court of the emperor and three from that of the prince. Having written to both of them, concerning my loss and difficult situation, and begging that anything saved from the wreck might be handed over to the captain and master of the ship, a servant of the prince came to visit me on his behalf and to hand over to me the keys of the warehouses where the goods were stored, so that I might do what I wished with them.

Since these events took place in the district that he governed, it was he who granted me this. Stripped as I was of all I owned, many would have taken advantage of this ruling, but it seemed to me better to cede my rights than to appropriate any part of the goods of so many poor and needy owners. Thus, I handed over the keys that I was given to the captain and master, so that he and the general could sell them or take them to Manila, whichever seemed best.

I then, as soon as I could, went to kiss the hands of the prince and his father for the kindness they had shown me, and they treated me with much honour and many marks of affection, as was made evident by their gifts. The prince gave me two swords, which they call *cathanas* like our scimitars or cutlasses[2], enriched with gold, and another ten of almost the same type, but shorter[3] in size. The emperor sent me twelve silk robes of the kind that are highly prized, which they call *quimones* and are worn in winter.

He also offered one of his ships, so that I may make my way to New Spain, as well as 3000 *taes*[4], and in the end I took advantage of this and returned by this means. I felt, however, that I was very heavily in his debt and kissed his hands for the generosity he had shown me and went on my way, travelling until I reached the port of Bungo, where the *Santa Ana* had docked.

Consecundono, the emperor's secretary, suggested that I should put before your Majesty a proposition to send some mining experts from New Spain, who would be treated with great generosity and favour, because they lose the advantage of many very rich mines through not knowing how to process the metal. He wanted me to let him know whether, while letters were going to Spain, the Viceroy could send them immediately on the first ship. Since I had already had my spurs on and was on the point of leaving, I told him that I would think what could be done and answer him from Miyako [Kyoto].

This is one of the largest cities in that kingdom, where a relative of Gotojosabrot[5], president of the emperor's Ministry of Finance, suggested on his own account and on behalf of other merchants, that they should build a ship in which I could travel to New Spain, on condition that I should make it possible for some merchants and merchandise to sail in it, because they wanted to learn the route of this trade which would be advantageous to both kingdoms. These negotiations were not so secret but that it was very soon clear that they were acting on the orders of the emperor. As soon as I was aware of this ruse, I was all the more convinced that we should face the situation and seize the opportunity, persuaded as I was by all the splendours of Japan which had attracted me. I gazed on them with great regret that your Majesty could not enjoy them, for without a doubt everything that I have seen in the world is nothing in comparison.

I decided, therefore, not to abandon the matter, nor to leave, although the season was far advanced, and it was agreed that the emperor would give permission to build a boat that would sail that year and I would go on it. They asked me for an answer to that which they had proposed regarding mining experts from New Spain. For the following reasons, I considered that I had a double obligation to serve your Majesty with love and faithfully, on the one hand this is right and proper in a subject and also in one belonging to your household.

God having led me, perhaps with some particular intention, to a place where I could never have foreseen or imagined my going, and having found myself with an opportunity that might not be offered again for centuries, I felt I should not let it pass without plucking some of the fruit. In view of what happened later, I soon realised that there would always be some clever person who would blame my excess of pure zeal in the service of Your Majesty, for the truth of it could not be hidden. Leaving this inconvenience aside, I only wished to move forward to open the doors to the greatest hopes that Your Majesty or any of your ancestors could have.

I wrote to the emperor, entrusting the friar, Father Luis de Sotelo of the Order of St Francis, with two copies of the letter addressed to Your Majesty. Essentially, it said that although I could not claim to know Your Majesty's royal wishes and expressed myself only cautiously, from what little I had understood, I believed that Your Majesty would be pleased that commercial and diplomatic relations should be established between the New World and Japan, given certain conditions and I put forward the most favourable terms that I could bring to mind. Once again, this meant, in essence, that Your Majesty would have entry wherever he wished, without being in any way committed, until the aims that I have mentioned have been achieved. Aims, the value of which I am absolutely convinced, as I do not believe any person would be in a position to refute or deny.

The priest, Fray Luis Sotelo, having delivered my letters, the emperor agreed to almost everything that I had proposed. He decided to send Fray Luis on an embassy to Your Majesty on a boat of his that he ordered to be prepared and I was told of this. Bearing in mind that one of things that would most concern Your Majesty and your ministers was the presence of the Dutch in the South Seas, so close to where Your Majesty's possessions lie, it seemed to me that matters were disposed in such a way that a good result might be obtained. Therefore, even though I had already set it down in writing, I decided to return to the court so as to deal with the matter more effectively face to face, for which purpose, I used asking permission to embark on his ship as an excuse and he was so well-pleased that in fact he sent for me; therefore, I was no longer able to continue my journey on board the *Santa Ana* as I had intended.

I reached the court of the emperor and immediately began to negotiate most hastily for the expulsion of the Dutch from the kingdom. He answered that he had given his word for this year, but in sending this ship it was clear that the friendship of a great a king such as your Majesty was more to be desired than that of people who lived by theft.

At this point, the emperor's ship took its departure and I was on it, together with the ambassadors and the gifts that he was sending to Your Majesty. To serve you was my only concern, without any other consideration in the world, and in order to do so I took upon myself the expenses of the ship, going four thousand ducats into debt to pay for the expenses of equipping it and, if it had been necessary for me to remain as security, as I have often said, I would have done so in exchange for this embassy reaching Your Majesty, since it would ensure tying the knot of friendship with the emperor, the advantages of which I will tell you in the following passages.

The first advantage, and that with the deepest foundations, is clearly the spiritual welfare of so many souls whom the ministers of the Holy Gospel are winning through their great zeal. Even if there were to be no hope of further gains, the preservation of the three hundred thousand Christians that there are in Japan and the risk of apostasy if they find themselves deprived of the support of the many churches and monasteries is, in the eyes of your most Christian Majesty, so powerful an argument that you would spend a good part of your royal patrimony to preserve it, considering good all means that tend to this one end. Since in Japan the will of kings is so respected and feared that one cannot walk but in their shadow, the emperor having declared that he wished a ship to leave for New Spain, any lukewarmness or delay on the part of the Christians in responding could well result in their disgrace and undoing in a few hours the gains of many years. Thus, on this most fundamental point, there has been no going backwards, but rather a good step forward, for with the sending of the ship, he has given what are called *chapas* and royal orders that priests may come and establish themselves publicly in all parts of Japan. Clearly, if up till now the Holy Gospel has been preached furtively and in secret, with the priests being forced to use a thousand stratagems and the seeking of favours[6] in order to overcome the difficulties the devil has set in their way, yet even so they have made three hundred thousand Christians. Now that they can proceed openly with the emperor's favour and his full permission, the growth will be so much the greater, as experience will show.

After this first most important and valuable consideration comes that of Your Majesty and the good of your kingdom. Peace treaties and alliances among kings are made for one of three reasons: for great hopes of some future plan, or to avoid some present danger to their army or navy on land or sea, or because they hope for some support or aid in order to make war on some nearby kingdom. All three reasons obtain regarding Japan. Truly, every servant or vassal who serves Your Majesty with love places his trust in the first of these designs, which are nourished by the greatest powers in the world[7].

Force of arms will not work in Japan. That which has worked in other parts of the world, thanks to the valour of the Spaniards, here cannot be attempted because of the great number of people who are both bellicose and brave, and because of the strength of their fortresses, some of which are completely unassailable. But that which is so difficult to obtain in this way is made easy through our first point: faith. For receiving it will open the eyes of these idolaters to the error in which they live and indeed they have no natural kings, and do not have them because all have imposed themselves as tyrants. Since the poor see themselves subjected to much poverty and oppression and the rich are so heavily taxed that they are not left sufficient sustenance to live, they clearly would appeal to a Christian king. And even, which may well be possible, they do not wish Your Majesty to be it [i.e.king], it would be very easy for whoever held this name to bring Your Majesty the support of 100 000 men to conquer the kingdom of Korea.

This country lies to the north at a height of 38°. It is *terra firma* and borders China to the west. Although there are a large number of inhabitants, they are rich and little inclined to war, for Taicosama, the predecessor of the present emperor of Japan conquered it almost entirely with 150 000 men and those whom he sent returned to the kingdom rich with the spoils they brought back. In good weather, you can go there from Japan in three days, because one of the islands of Japan is forty leagues from Surunga, the seat of the emperor's court, and from there it is another fifty leagues.

The Japanese who provided this information told me that although the people of Korea are very numerous, they are known to be timid and cowardly and with a reasonable number of Spaniards and some help from the Japanese, obtained through an alliance with whichever emperor might be in power, it would be very easy to conquer this land. This would provide Your Majesty with more income than any other of your kingdoms because it is so rich in gold and silver and has many products similar to those of Spain, as well as great places with the houses built of solid masonry. And once our feet are there, our arms can stretch as far as China, the vast extent of which Your Majesty is well aware.

The second point concerning the damage which the armies and navies of kings can receive as a reason for alliances with neighbouring countries undoubtedly has more relevance in this case than in any other, because if the emperor of Japan were your enemy, Your Majesty could not sail a ship from Spain anywhere in the Southern Seas. If the Dutch were to ally themselves with them and held a port in Japan, they would be able to sally out safely to await the ships from New Spain heading for the Philippines. In less than fifteen days they would be able to bar the entrance to Capul and to Cape Bojeador[8], so that not a bird could enter or leave for any destination, so the Philippines would be lost and likewise the trade that they have with New Spain.

After discussing so serious a detriment, is it necessary to mention yet another? The ships sailing from Manila to New Spain are often forced, through storms or other urgent reasons, to land on the coasts of Japan, something often impossible to avoid given its position, and so putting in jeopardy the lives and goods of those who travel on them.

An equally important consideration is the strength which the Dutch could draw in order to make war on Your Majesty in Terranate[9], since they could obtain all kinds of supplies from Japan – ships' biscuit, rice, meat, etc. and apart from this everything they would need for their maintenance and expansion because they could obtain large quantities of copper and cast iron, gunpowder, munitions, cordage and, above all, build ships, careen and repair them better than in any other part of the world and even dispose of many of the spices of Terranate, since the journey is so short that in 20 days it is possible to cross from one part to the other.

The third reason for which kings ask each other for assistance in their wars is connected with what I said to Your Majesty concerning Korea and it would be good to make such provision, even if so large a scale project is never carried out. Taking the opportunity now to establish a presence in a Japanese port and continuing in friendship with the emperor would fulfil the first of these aims.

I would like to remind Your Majesty that in order to maintain the Moluccas, it is necessary to impoverish the Philippines, which are bled and drained of men, ships and money, all things that could serve to fortify and strengthen people of the state. As things are today, every year the Moluccas need more than a hundred or a hundred and fifty men and the 15 000 baskets of rice and 130 000 pesos normally taken from here to support them are not sufficient. Furthermore, to bring them this aid, three ships are needed, because the Dutch are prowling about the area and it was only by a miracle that in my time, we escaped from their hands and I cannot guarantee that under Juan de Silva some unfortunate event will not occur.

The small number of Indians to be found today in the Philippines, are so harassed by these fleets for the Moluccas that unless something is done they will vanish altogether, or else rebel. Your Majesty has the remedy to all these problems by establishing a presence in a Japanese port and bringing soldiers there each year from New Spain who could go on to the Moluccas with only half the expenditure in rice and sea biscuit. And if artillery were needed, metal could be found with which to make it and ammunition and even powder, although it is not as good as that of New Spain, in spite of the saltpetre being excellent.

It would be very easy to establish ship yards there to build ships and galleys and in no part of the world would they be better made nor at less cost. The expense Your Majesty is at to bring rope, iron and cordage from the port of Acapulco would be almost entirely spared, because in Japan these things cost very little. Thus, as I understand it, with what Your Majesty would save with these new routes, there would be enough money to pay for the sending of a boat each year from New Spain to Japan. Again, the Philippines would be able to rest without having to shoulder the burden of sending ships to Terranate. Also the boats would be able to enter by a better route and would be safer from the enemy, since they are bringing cloves and spices from the Moluccas, being the profit which that country has to offer and the reason for which it was conquered.

Your Majesty could, then, have this merchandise taken from there to Japan and from there to New Spain. I am not one of those who maintain that there would be no profit in the trade between New Spain and Japan, nor do I want to give Your Majesty dubious information on matters which time will soon clarify, but it is quite certain that Japan has an abundance of silver and gold, which is no poor return for cloth, cochineal and indigo, leather, felt, blankets and other goods which are well-liked and very necessary. Both Spain and the Indies have these things in such abundance that they can be sent from there with very adequate profit. And if the Philippines send taffeta, cheap plates and bowls to the value of the million and a half which are taken there every year, and this system is maintained and preserved, all the more reason to esteem Japan, which will take that which is useless to us and send back that which is so profitable.

This is particularly true since Your Majesty will enter this exchange without any of the excessive expenditure, which has followed other new discoveries. Questions could be asked and doubts raised, but since it is Your Majesty who receives and nothing is given from your house, I do not see what there can be against it. At the most, friendship with the emperor will require that every year a ship be sent from Acapulco, as it is from Manila. Its going not from the Philippines but from New Spain, will cause no inconvenience of any kind, because every year five or six of the ships which they call *juncos* go from Japan to Manila for the trade in raw silk which the Spaniards of that city send off, receiving lard and other things of little importance in exchange. There is plenty for everyone in this trade and enough ships without it being necessary for Your Majesty's ships to sail from there.

But I think that considering the matter well, it will be clear that there are officials more concerned with their own gains than with whether Your Majesty would lose by sending it [the ship]. For this reason, there is much opposition in the city, the *Audiencia* and from the governor, because they all have vested interests and, although the governor does not have mercantile concerns, he is deeply involved in matters of jurisdiction and for this reason is opposed to its passing to New Spain[10].

Although wood is more expensive in the port of Acapulco, this ship can always be provisioned with everything needful in Japan where, as we have already said, things are more easily available than in the Philippines. The little that the ship will cost can easily be recovered – and indeed the money will be more than enough – from the dues on merchandise to be paid by the persons lading the vessel in New Spain.

Inevitably, there will be people who say that Your Majesty should feel insulted by what happened with the Macao ship and also that they held on to a greater or lesser amount of goods that washed up on the beach from the *San Francisco* and that in such times alliances should not be made with the emperor. I do not know whether those who take this view have looked at the causes with the sober consideration that the service of Your Majesty demands, because in both cases, as one who was a witness and played an active part, I maintain that the emperor's role was blameless.

It all began in Macao where, for many years, there had been a continuous, normal and unbroken peace with Japan; then more than two hundred men, including ambassadors, had their throats cut. They had been sent to the kingdom of Champam[11], but were driven there in a storm and instead of being treated with honour and welcomed as guests they were killed and their possessions stolen. It was an outrage as great as that of the captain of the Macao galleon, who did not choose to obey the emperor, even when he sent for him twice to explain the reason why this had happened. Because of his refusal to obey, the emperor sent to capture him and since he resisted this too they burned the ship and Your Majesty knows what happened.

As regards the chests and goods from the *San Francisco*, as I have already written to Your Majesty, as soon as the prince and emperor received my letters, they gave orders that it should be handed over and everything was handed over that had been collected up. As regards any thefts and pilfering which occurred, I believe the responsibility lies with the *Capitán General* and the ship's Master who, in charge of bringing in the ship and its goods, left everything unprotected on the beach where the chests were being carried in, not setting two guards to watch over them, the blame is with them rather than with the emperor, who conceded everything that was asked of him, without refusing anything.

And even if it is considered that there is some reason for blaming the emperor, although I do not think there is in either of these two cases, it should be considered what Your Majesty loses in losing such a friend and not having this alliance could prove so harmful it seems to me, insofar as I understand it, that it is neither opportune to complain nor show any feeling in the matter. Your Majesty can see that these people want to justify with reason the actions of their prince in his court. The General of the Sea was sent to me with all the details I have mentioned so that we might be satisfied regarding the Macao ship, so that I might inform Your Majesty, as indeed I have done, truthfully and punctually, as the service I owe Your Majesty.

As regards the greatness of Japan and its importance to Your Majesty and the question of how to draw closer to that country and foster the friendship with the emperor, there is much to say, but I am afraid of wearying Your Majesty with so much material and such a long letter. For this alone, I would come to your royal presence, but poor health and stricken by many difficulties – for although I did not have much, I lost it all on the *San Francisco* – I have been compelled to bury myself in my corner and live on a very tight budget until Your Majesty, as I hope, chooses to reward my work and services, some of which have been considerable. Among other things, I would like to set before Your Majesty the fact that I went into debt in order to equip the ship that came from the emperor, so that the embassy sent to Your Majesty would not fail in its mission.

Although the emperor had previously ordered an envoy to be sent, afterwards the expense seemed great, which cooled their enthusiasm until I came. I could only get them to agree to it on condition that I contribute the crew, sails and rigging and that I should return it [the ship], or, alternatively, in case Your Majesty did not wish to pay the cost of sending it back, it could be sold for the best possible price and the proceeds invested in various kinds of merchandise, of which they would give me a memorandum. These would be taken to the Philippines; together with the Japanese who were travelling on the ship, and from there they could return to their own country.

I told the various Orders and priests and monks in Japan about the situation, explaining that I was naked, stripped of all resources.

I was not thinking so much about the question of taking such a great burden on my own shoulders, as about Your Majesty's royal prestige. Since I bore the title of your minister and a member of your household and, having served you in a position highly respected in Japan, that of Governor of the Philippines, it seemed unfitting that I should back out at the last minute, lest these barbarians should form a low opinion of the majesty of Spain and its affairs. It was really this that tipped the balance, rather than my shortness of cash and if need be, I would even have put myself up for auction. I therefore came and asked to borrow three thousand five hundred ducats from their strong box. This, the Fathers of the Order of San Francisco who were staying there very generously gave me and together we signed an undertaking to send back the Japanese on the first available ship. This was done in the manner I have explained.

The Viceroy of New Spain should understand, as he consults Your Majesty, that all the great hopes for Japan and for the Christian faith established there today will be lost if the relationship, financial and otherwise, is not sound. And I have no doubt that he will do what might be expected from one of his sagacity, just as he has begun with the honour and warm welcome that he has shown the Japanese. Not only the certainty of good treatment which, as foreigners, they deserve to receive from Your Majesty and his ministers, but also to repay the generosity they showed to me in the name of Your Majesty: both require a most generous demonstration of hospitality and gifts.

The Father Commissary, Fray Alonso Muñoz, was the person finally appointed ambassador and he will bring Your Majesty the presents from the emperor. He is a monk with great qualities, both personal and in terms of leadership, and will also bring the gifts from the prince as well as the *chapas* and Royal Ordinances conceded by the emperor.

Lastly, I beg Your Majesty not too lose such a magnificent opportunity, the greatest perhaps to be offered in many centuries, but rather to order that fifty married men should be sent out to settle in the port, together with a number of priests and monks who will go forth, their blood hot, delighting in this great occasion for rejoicing.

And, furthermore, let some gentleman, who is both shrewd and absolutely trustworthy, bring gifts and settle this new agreement with the emperor, as well as the one relating to the mines and the mining experts, which if well carried out could most privately provide Your Majesty with a very large income. It seems to me that this is the most important enterprise that Your Majesty is engaged in these parts and that the same man could be employed as he who governs the Philippines. It does not seem to me that that would be a mistake and, furthermore, in order to govern them better, before taking up the post, a couple of years in Japan would be an excellent experience. It is by the matter of a good move or a leaden one that these first negotiations will stand or fall. Since Your Majesty is so far away and cannot easily be consulted on new events that may arise, much prudence is required of those who must take decisions concerning them. The Viceroys of New Spain should keep a firm hand on matters concerning Japan, with Your Majesty's permission

As to what is done about returning this boat, I will inform Your Majesty by the first ship that leaves and since this matter was my concern, I am very sorry to be neither sufficiently at ease nor sufficiently rich to be able, without the aid of the Viceroy, to send the ship back to the emperor, together with his subjects, for there would be such delight at this that they [the Japanese] would make no difficulties over anything that might be asked of them. If I manage to find the wherewithal to cover my nakedness, I will cross with the fleet and tell Your Majesty of these matters, otherwise, I will set it down clearly in writing, deeply regretting that I cannot do this service for Your Majesty in person.

The Marques de Salinas has told me that a decree has been granted for an expedition to the Isle Rich in Silver. I am of a different opinion to that which has been put forward to obtain Your Majesty's consent. This island may well be imaginary – no one has ever seen it – and no one knows whether or not here is a harbour, nor anything about the land. It is thought to lie a hundred and fifty leagues from Japan, but well before they reach it, the ships bound for the Philippines will already have endured such storms and other dangers that they meet and in case of dire necessity will have no need to go so far. Japan is supplied with a thousand ports abundantly provided everything that could be wanted in the way of cordage, wood and provisions. If it would be judged convenient for ships to stop along the way, as I understand it, Japan, which is being offered to Your Majesty, is the place most fitting and in any case there is no other.

In addition to this, even if they should favour this project in spite of so many arguments against it, it would obviously be very dangerous to carry it out at the present time. It is so close to Japan that, seeing ships go out on new voyages of discovery, the emperor could get the impression that they were being sent against him to make war. This could break the peace that is of such importance to us and has such sure foundations. Thus, in mid-summer and without it costing two thousand pesos, it would be possible to set out from Japan to discover these islands, see what they hold and inform Your Majesty – may God keep him and may He grant him life for the increase of the Holy Faith and the growth and extension of his kingdoms.

From this the port of Matanchel, in the province of Guadalaxara, on the twenty-seventh of October in the year one thousand six hundred and ten.

Don Roderigo de Vivero

1   *Capitán General de la Armada* – the person in charge of the defence of the convoy of ships in the Carrera de Indias.
2   *Alfage*
3   "*…puestas en unas medias picas*"- perhaps the short sword, *wakizashi*, that, with the *katana*, makes up the *daishō*, or official set of arms worn by the samurai.
4   Portuguese *taeis*, plural of *tael*, used across the Far East, especially China, but also Japan for a unit of roughly 40gr of silver.
5   Unidentified.
6   *Imbendiciones*
7   This phrase is somewhat obscure.
8   The name was calked on Acapulco and Capul in the Philippines was a fortified town with an important lighthouse, built to guide the Manila galleons through the treacherous San Bernardino Strait. Cape Bojeador at Burgos in Ilocos Norte in the Philippines had another important lighthouse, although the structure there today dates from the 19th century.
9   Ternate – one of the spice islands in the Moluccas.
10 Not surprisingly, Vivero is perfectly correct in his analysis – see Introduction.
11 Cham Kingdom (present-day South and central Vietnam); in the *Relacion*, Vivero mentions ambassadors to Siam – see Introduction.

Glossary

Alcalde: A member of a municipal government with administrative and judicial functions (often functioned as a judge).

Alférez: Traditionally a military position in the Middle Ages, usually synonymous with standard-bearer or leader of the King's private army. It is often translated Lieutenant, however, in the Indies the position was largely ceremonial, and it became a symbolic and hereditary title that represented the military presence of the Crown in the sphere of municipal government.

Alguacil mayor: Chief constable, on a municipal level. At the time when the office could be bought for life it also included some direct political power, as it included the privilege of a vote in the town council (*cabildo*).

*Audiencia Real (*usually *Real Audiencia):* These were high tribunals to which all of criminal and civil sentences in a given territory could be sent for appeal. They were modelled, in the Indies, on the *Real Audiencias y Chancillerías* of Valladolid and Granada. In the territories where there did not exist a Viceroyalty, such as in the Caribbean, they also exercised supreme administrative and political authority, and were subordinate only to the *Consejo de Indias* in Spain.

Capitán General de Tierra Firme: Capitanías were in general given to individuals as rewards for their efforts in conquering new territories in the Indies. They amounted to gubernatorial positions – often intended to be for life. The position of *Capitán General de Tierra Firme* was first created and granted to Pedro Arias de Avila (usually known as Pedrarias Dávila) in 1513, in recognition of his conquest of *Tierra Firme*, or the Isthmus of Panama.

Carrera de Indias: The maritime route linking Spain with its overseas colonies.

Cédulas: Decrees

Consejo de Indias: or *Real y Supremo Consejo de Indias*, the main administrative body for Spanish possessions in the Americas and Asia, formally constituted in 1524.

Diligencia: Procedure

General: which can refer to the naval commander *Capitán General de la Armada*, which was the person in charge of the defence of the convoy of ships in the *Carrera de Indias*.

Presidente de la Real Audiencia: The head of the *Audiencia*, and as such, often a judge.

Provisiones reales: Royal ordinances

[see dialnet.unirioja.es/descarga/articulo/241012.pdf for details]

Tierra Firme: Or *Provincia de Tierra Firme* comprised the Isthmus of Panama and the adjoining mainland areas, now in Columbia and Venezuela, as opposed to the Caribbean.

Index

Lightning Source UK Ltd.
Milton Keynes UK
UKOW06n1442250615

254116UK00004B/54/P